Contents

Also available in the
Wise Guides series:

BULLYING
Michele Elliott

DIVORCE AND SEPARATION
Matthew Whyman

DRUGS
Anita Naik

PERIODS
Charlotte Owen

SELF-ESTEEM
Anita Naik

SEX
Anita Naik

YOUR RIGHTS

Anita Naik

Illustrated by Harry Venning

*Hodder
Children's
Books*

a division of Hodder Headline plc

Text copyright 1999 © Anita Naik
Illustrations copyright 1999 © Harry Venning
Published by Hodder Children's Books 1999

Design by Fiona Webb

The rights of Anita Naik and Harry Venning to be identified as the author
and illustrator of the work have been asserted by them in
accordance with the Copyright, Designs and Patents Act 1988.

10 9 8 7 6 5 4 3 2 1

ISBN: 0 340 74419 7

The information in this book has been thoroughly researched
and checked for accuracy. Neither the author nor the publisher
can accept any responsibility for any loss, injury or damage
incurred as a result of using this book.

Printed by The Guernsey Press Company Limited,Guernsey,C.I.

Hodder Children's Books
a division of Hodder Headline plc
338 Euston Road
London NW1 3BH

Introduction

Laws, rules, regulations, restrictions - as a teenager it feels like the main purpose of people in authority is to spoil your fun and curb your pleasure. However, the law's purpose isn't to stop you from having a good time. Believe it or not, it's there to protect you. Protect you from what you might ask? Well, for starters from things like harmful substances, exploitative adults, dangerous pursuits and even yourself.

It's also there to give you rights. Such as the right to an education, health care, a clean environment, and the right to walk down the street without being abused.

If these don't feel like rights, then imagine a world without them. A world where you, and anyone else, could do whatever you wanted, whenever you wanted. Imagine how much crime there would be then, how you'd have to fight for all the things you probably take for granted right now. Scary thought, isn't it?

Having rights also means you have the power to do something if you feel you're being unfairly treated or exploited. Of course, if you're anything like the kind of teenager I was, it's unlikely you'll know this kind of information and even if you do, you're probably unsure about what to do with it. So this is what this Wise Guide is all about. A guide to your rights, and what to do with them, so you can ensure you get the most out of your life, whatever you choose to do.

Anita

Your Rights

The laws in the majority of this book apply to England and Wales, not Scotland and Northern Ireland which have their own legal systems. While certain areas like drug laws and parental responsibility are very similar (if not the same), there are significant differences in many other laws. We have outlined the main differences. For more information, advice and help for laws regarding Northern Ireland and Scotland, and also for the Republic of Ireland, please contact the Child Law Centres, listed at the back of the book.

This book is intended as a general guide only. For accessibility, non-legal language has been used. The organisations listed in this book will be able to provide up-to-date information (as all laws are subject to change) and the precise wording of the laws where necessary.

The author and publishers would like to thank the Children's Legal Centre for their help and expert advice.

CHAPTER ONE

Your Health

L ooking after your health isn't always as simple as going to the doctor every time you feel sick. For starters, it's not just about seeking help when you get ill. It's also about prevention, in other words making sure you don't put your health at risk – by taking something that will hurt you, like drugs for example. Or by having something done to yourself, like a tattoo in an unregistered salon. This is why laws exist to protect you from harming yourself.

However, when it comes to your health, you also have many rights, even if you're under 16. Like the right to privacy and, in some cases, the right to say no to treatment.

You may think you already know all these rights, but even the most together person is unlikely to be 100% sure of what kind of help they're entitled to, and what their parents can and can't make them do when it comes to looking after their health.

Your Health Rights

- You have the right to be registered with a doctor.
- You have the right to change doctors.
- You have the right to complain officially about a doctor/dentist.
- If you are under 16 (or under 19 and still in full time education) you have the right to free dental treatments, eye tests, and prescriptions.
- You have the right to confidentiality (see p5).
- You have the right to ask for information.
- You are entitled to emergency care.
- You have the right to express your opinion about medical treatment.

MEDICAL TREATMENT

What the words mean

consent to give permission

competent able to understand what is going on

'Competency'

"How come doctors who don't even know you have the right to decide whether you're grown up enough or not to say yes or no to an operation?"

Vic (14)

People over the age of 16 are seen by the law as being 'competent', in other words, able to consent (agree) to their own medical treatment, because it is generally agreed that they will understand what's going on and any possible consequences of their treatment.

However, if you're under 16, the law sees you as a child, and so assumes you are not competent, which means you're unable to consent to your own treatment.

Before you give up in despair and never visit the doctor again, though, there is a ruling that often works in favour of under 16s. The Gillick Ruling, 1985, states that people under 16 who are able to fully understand what is proposed and its implications *are* competent to consent to medical treatment regardless of age.

This means doctors can provide you with medical treatment (depending on exactly what the treatment is) if you're under the age of 16 without your parents' agreement, if you are competent and consent. The decision as to whether or not you may be competent is down to your doctor. Obviously, this is a very unclear area because the decision is a personal one. However, the older you are, the more likely a doctor is to find you competent.

'Consent'

UNDER 16

"If I really don't want something done to me at the doctor's, can I say no?"

Ellie (12)

Saying no to treatment
If your doctor thinks you are competent – that you understand what's going on, why it's happening and what the treatment entails – this means you can say no to treatment. However, in practice, it's unlikely a doctor will allow you to refuse treatment without seeking parental consent, especially if you are putting your life at risk.

If you and your parents disagree over treatment, and you are considered to be competent, you can independently seek medical advice and give consent to medical treatment without your parents' consent.

When parental consent is needed
* When you want treatment and the doctor decides you are incompetent. If this happens you will need the consent of the parent who has

parental responsibility over you (see page 47).
(It's unnecessary to get both your parents to give
consent.)
- For the donation of your organs.

16 YEARS AND OVER

Once over the age of sixteen, you are the only one
who can say whether or not you want an examination
or treatment with your GP, dentist or at a hospital.
This means your parents cannot make you do
anything you don't want to do, without going to
court and making you a ward of court.

However, your consent is not necessary in an
emergency – if you've been in an accident, for example.

'Confidentiality'

What the words mean

confidentiality this means the information you have
given is secret and no-one else can read it, hear about it
or know about it, without your consent

All adult patients have the right to confidentiality and believe it or not, so too do teenagers. This means you have the right to consult any doctor and know that whatever you say will be kept between you and him or her. Even if a doctor says no to what you want – contraception for example (see chapter 4) – they cannot tell your parents why you have come to see them, unless it is an emergency situation. However, bear in mind that a doctor will undoubtedly try to persuade you to tell your parents yourself.

Confidentiality also means that you don't have to go along to the doctor with your parents and your parents do not have to be present during an examination.

Complaints

If you're unhappy with your treatment or with something that's happened at the surgery, start by trying to discuss matters with the GP in question or the person in charge of the surgery (known as the practice manager). All surgeries have an in-house complaints procedure, so ask for details of that.

If you don't want to discuss it with the surgery, or feel the problem has gone beyond that, go to your local Community Health Council (ring 0171 609 8405 to find out your local number). You have to take action within a year of the event.

If a doctor does something unethical, it mean he or she's gone against the medical moral code, and done something inappropriate. If you believe a GP has behaved unethically or is incompetent, you and your parents can report him/her to the General Medical Council (0171 580 7642).

If you have been harmed by treatment and want to take the matter to court, contact Action for Victims of Medical Accidents 0181 291 2793, for details.

Privacy and your GP

"When I have to go to the doctor for a check up, does my mum always have to stand in the room and answer all the questions for me? It's so embarrassing."

Jack (12)

Most people feel very private about their bodies and their health and because of this, it can be tempting to not tell a doctor the whole truth during an examination. Your mum or dad may realise that and so want to help you out, even though if you are considered competent, they do not have to be present by law.

While no-one can make you tell all (not even the law), there are good reasons why you should always be honest with your doctor. The questions may seem nosy, silly or useless, but don't be vague about your answers. They are important otherwise he/she wouldn't bother to ask you. If you lie, this can be dangerous to your health. Doctors are there to help you and they can only do this if you tell them all the facts.

Don't be afraid to ask questions about anything you don't understand no matter how stupid you may think your questions are.

Where to go if you don't want to see your GP

In certain situations you may not want to see your GP or go to your local surgery. Maybe you're worried you're pregnant, or have an STI (Sexually Transmitted Infection) or you want contraception (see chapter 4 for more details). If this is the case you can also visit a Brook Advisory Clinic, a Family Planning Youth Clinic or a Genito Urinary Clinic. Brook Advisory Centres offer free, confidential birth control advice to under 16s. Likewise, Family Planning Clinics offer a similar service and are free to anyone on the NHS. The doctors at these clinics have to adhere to the same rules and regulations your GP does.

Changing your GP

It can often be hard to see your family doctor as someone who can help you with private problems.

Perhaps you feel he/she may 'disapprove' or will tell your parents. Or maybe you want to see a female doctor because you feel too embarrassed to have a male doctor examine your body.

If this is the case, then it's perfectly within your rights to change doctors (though you'll have to tell your parents you're changing doctors, just in case there is ever an emergency). You can change your GP for any reason whatsoever, and you don't have to tell anyone why. All you have to do is find another GP surgery and ask them to take you on.

So how do you choose a doctor? Start by asking your friends, school nurse, your parents or an adult you trust for a recommendation. As long as you live in the same area as the doctor you want to change to and he/she has some space on their books, there should be no problem. When you find a doctor you like just take along your medical card (if you have one) and ask to be taken on.

Getting a dentist

As you have the right to free dental care if you're under 16 (or 16–19 but still in full time education), you also have the right to a dentist. Your District Dental Officer may be able to help you find a dentist in your area. Look under District Health Service in your telephone directory. The Family Health Services Authority will have a list of all dentists registered under the NHS in your area.

Getting an optician

If you are under 16 (or 16–19 but still in full time education) you are entitled to free eye tests and vouchers towards glasses.

LAWS PROTECTING YOUR HEALTH

Body piercing and tattoos

BODY PIERCING

At present there is no law which stops a person under 18 from having a body piercing, but technically a piercer who goes ahead without parental permission is committing an assault, which is why reputable piercers do ask under 18s for proof of parental consent. Reputable piercers are also required by law to be licensed by the local health authority in terms of safety and hygiene (ask to see a displayed certificate). The Department of Health does this to ensure that the strictest standards of hygiene are applied, so that blood borne (passed through blood) viruses such as HIV and hepatitis B and C are not transmitted to people.

TATTOOS

Legally, you cannot have a tattoo until you have reached the age of 18 (Tattooing of Minors Act 1969). This is because tattoos are permanent, and very painful to remove if you feel you've made a mistake.

Reputable tattooists will not tattoo you unless you have proof you are aged 18 or over. If you're tempted to go to a place that tattoos under 18s consider the fact that if the tattooist is willing to break the law, it's likely he/she is not registered with your local authority and may be putting you at risk from anything from HIV to hepatitis.

Alcohol

"I suspect my older sister and her friends are drinking. There's always a weird smell of wine in her room and on their breath. They're only 15 years old. Can they do this?"
Mark (14)

Even though drinking alcohol is not illegal as such, it is very dangerous in large amounts. Whether it's fair or not, the law says that young people cannot always be trusted to be sensible about drinking and therefore need to be protected.

If you think this is rubbish, consider the fact that over 1000 under 15s are taken to hospital every year with acute alcohol poisoning. Drinking alcohol regularly also increases the risk of developing certain diseases and can damage your brain, liver, stomach and mental health.

RESTRICTIONS ON ALCOHOL (see also chapter 7)

Classification of alcohol

All alcoholic drinks have to be labelled with the percentage of alcohol contained within the bottle. This can help you to compare strengths and not get drunk when you drink.

The percentage can range from 40% for whiskey to 1% for low alcohol wine. It's important to note the so called alco-pops – alcoholic lemonade etc. – are fairly high at 5%.

What the words mean

prosecuted taken to court for breaking the law

BUYING ALCOHOL

Attempting to buy, or buying, alcohol under the age of 18, is not allowed by law. If you are aged between 14 and 17, you can be fined up to £1000 for trying to buy a drink on licensed premises (a pub or restaurant).

If you are aged between 10 and 13, the fine is £250.

Pub landlords and shopkeepers who sell alcohol to someone under the age of 18 could also be prosecuted.

ALCOHOL AND YOUR PARENTS

The law is also very clear on adults buying or selling you alcohol. Your parents or older friends will be committing a criminal offence if they buy you a drink in a bar or send you out to buy alcohol if you are under 18.

However, you are allowed beer or cider if you are over 16 and in a restaurant with an adult. And under the eyes of the law it is not an offence to drink in your own home (once you are over the age of 5 years) or someone else's, so your parents are not breaking the law if they give you alcohol at home.

Smoking

RESTRICTIONS ON SMOKING

While some people think it looks fashionable and cool to smoke, buying cigarettes is restricted to over 16s because it has been medically proved that smoking can seriously damage your health. The statistics below are just a small indication why the government seeks to protect children from buying and smoking cigarettes.

- Smoking kills around six times more people in the UK than road and other accidents, murder, suicide and diseases.
- Half of all regular smokers will eventually be killed by their habit.
- Smoking causes 1 in 3 of all cancer deaths (including 90% of lung cancer deaths).
- Tobacco contains over 4000 chemicals, including nicotine which is addictive and tar which is deposited in the lungs.

Therefore the law states:

- It is an offence for a shop keeper to sell cigarettes to a person under 16, whether they are for their own use or not. This includes cigarette papers, cigars and tobacco.
- While it is not against the law to smoke at any age, a police officer can take away cigarettes from any person under 16 seen to be smoking in a public place.

PASSIVE SMOKING

Passive smoking – the inhaling of secondary smoke from someone who is smoking around you – causes several hundred people to die every year from lung cancer. While at present there is no law to protect an individual from this, the Government's Scientific Committee on Tobacco and Health has acknowledged that passive smoking leads to several hundred lung cancer deaths in the UK each year. This in turn has led the Department of the Environment to publish a Code of Practice on controlling smoking in public places.

SMOKING IN THE HOME AND AT WORK

While there are no laws which deal with smoking in the home, there are several laws which will cover you and your parents when you go out to work.

- *Common Law*
  Under Common Law, people who suffer illness as a result of passive smoking have the right to sue their employers for damages.
- *The Health and Safety at Work Act 1974*
  The Health and Safety at Work Act says it is your employer's duty to provide a safe working environment, without risks to your health.
- *European Union Directives*
  Under European Union Directives, rest areas must have separate smoking and non-smoking areas.

Drugs

Apart from the obvious fact that drugs can kill you, they are also extremely harmful to your everyday health (see next page), which is why they are illegal and carry severe penalties if you are caught with them (see chapter 7).

DRUG	HEALTH RISK
Cannabis	Affects short term memory, increases the risk of accidents due to impaired state of mind.
Cocaine	Heart problems, chest pain, paranoia and depression.
Anabolic Steroids	Stunted growth. Substantial risks for men, including: erection problems, breast growth, increased risk of heart attack. In women: growth of facial hair, deepening voice.

Ecstasy	Increase in heart rate, depression, possibly death.
Glues/Gases/Aerosol	Instant death, fatal heart problems, blackouts and brain, liver and kidney damage.
Speed	Depression, hallucinations, strain on the heart and sleep problems.
Cigarettes	Contain over 4000 chemicals which are harmful to health. Cause cancer and heart disease.

THE MISUSE OF DRUGS ACT

Under this act, drugs are divided into three classes (alcohol, gases, glues, aerosols and cigarettes are not handled under this act, but dealt with separately) to determine how the law responds to a person found handling them.

Class A Drugs
cocaine, crack, Ecstasy, heroin, LSD, Magic Mushrooms, speed (if prepared for injection).

Maximum penalties:
for possession – 7 years and a fine
for supply – life imprisonment and a fine

Class B Drugs
cannabis, speed

Maximum penalties:
for possession – 5 years and a fine
for supply – 14 years and a fine

Class C Drugs
tranquillisers

Maximum penalties:
for possession – 2 years and a fine
for supply – 5 years and a fine

Remember, if you have a drugs conviction your employers in the future are likely to find out about it and it may affect your employment chances.

THE MEDICINES ACT

Many of the drugs that are not mentioned in the Misuse of Drugs Act are controlled by the Medicines Act. This means while it isn't illegal to possess such drugs – ketamine or GHB for example – to supply them is still an offence.

For instance, Anabolic steroids (often used for training and sports purposes) can be sold lawfully by a pharmacist to someone with a doctor's prescription. However, if this person then gives the steroids to someone else, in other words supplies them with the drug, he or she is breaking the law and Class C penalties from the Misuse of Drugs Act apply (see above).

GASES, GLUES AND AEROSOLS

The number of household products that fall into this category is huge, and because of their widespread domestic use, it's impossible to make them illegal.

The Intoxicating Substances Supply Act 1985 makes it an offence to supply a person under 18 with a substance which traders feel might be used for intoxication.

Questions and answers

I find going to the doctor's really embarrassing and would prefer to see a female doctor. The problem is my family doctor is a man. Can I change doctors?

Leah (13)

These days because most surgeries are group practices (this means you can see any of the doctors who work within the surgery) it's very easy to ask for an appointment with a female doctor. Usually you won't be asked why, but if you are, just say you'd feel more comfortable seeing a woman. If there is no female doctor working at your surgery, then tell your parents you'd like to change to another surgery. As long as you live in the same area as the doctor you want to change to and she has some space on her books, there should be no problem.

I read in the paper that lots of under 16s have been able to get body piercings. If this is the case, how come magazines and books always say you have to be over 16 or get parental permission to get your body pierced?

Laura (14)

Unlike for tattoos, there is no law telling body piercers they can't pierce an under 18. However, good, above-board piercers do always ask for parental permission, to make sure your parents won't later try to sue them and to prove that you can all be assured that the strictest standards of hygiene will be applied. Always be wary of piercers who don't ask your age, or don't have high levels of hygiene. Body piercing with a dirty needle can give you any number of diseases.

INFORMATION AND ADVICE

The Children's Legal Centre publish a full guide to Confidentiality which is available from them (see p143 for address).

Health

Department of Health
Richmond House
79 Whitehall
London SW1A 2NL
Tel: 0171 210 5983

Young Minds
22A Boston Place
London NW1 6ER
Tel: 0171 724 7262

Drugs

Narcotics Anonymous
PO Box 1980
London N19 3LS
Tel: 0171 351 6794.
Self-help group for drug users.

Adfam National
82 Old Brompton Road
London SW7 3LQ
Tel: 0171 823 9313
A national helpline supplying help and advice for the
family and friends of drug users.

Release
388 Old Street
London EC1V 9LT
Tel: 0171 603 8654
For details of local drug counselling agencies in
your area.

Alcohol

Alateen
61 Great Dover Street
London SE1 4YF
Tel: 0171 403 0888

Al-Anon
Family Groups
61 Great Dover Street
London SE1 4YF

Drinkline
0345 320202

Alcoholics Anonymous
Head Office
PO Box 1
Stonebow House
Stonebow
York YO1 2NJ
Tel: 01904 644026

Alcohol Concern
Waterbridge House
32–36 Lonman Street
London SE1 0EE
Tel: 0171 928 7377

Smoking

Quit (National Society of Non-Smokers)
102 Gloucester Place
London W1H 3DA
Tel: 0171 487 3000 (helpline)

Ash (Action on Smoking and Health)
109 Gloucester Place,
London W1H 3PH.
Tel: 0171 935 3519

CHAPTER TWO

Your Education

Education, schoolwork, teachers, homework, exams – does the thought of all these make you feel ill? Does the idea that you must go to school seem unfair and unjust? Would you rather just stay at home all day?

Well, if your answer is – yes – to all of the above, imagine a world where education wasn't available or where only people with money could become educated.

How unfair would that be? Not only would you not be able to read and write but also you wouldn't be able to get a good job and the benefits that come with that.

Education is now considered a basic human right, and as a young person you are entitled to it. What's more, it is compulsory for under 16s.

Your Education Rights

- You have the right to be educated at a school (until 19).
- You have the right to leave school at 16 (for more details see section on leaving school).
- You have the right not to be abused/bullied at school by a teacher.

EDUCATION

What the words mean

compulsory you have to, you have no choice

Going to school

Under the 1996 Education Act it is compulsory for you to be educated from the age of 5 years. Your parents have to therefore make sure you are receiving a full time education somewhere – either at home or at a school. It is a criminal offence for them not to do this.

In Scotland you have to start school between the ages of 4 years and 6 months and 5 years and 3 months. In N. Ireland, you have to start school at the age of 4 years.

Leaving school

"Can I leave school whenever I want?"

Pete (12)

You have to stay in full time education if you are under the age of 16, after which it is up to you whether to choose to stay on, or leave.

This doesn't mean you can just stop going to school on your 16th birthday. You can leave at the end of Year 11 provided you'll be 16, if you aren't already, before school starts again in September.

Staying on at school

Under the Further and Higher Education Act 1992 you do not have to leave school at the end of Year 11, and are entitled to free full time education at schools, technical colleges and sixth form colleges up to the age of 19.

Choosing a school

Your parents can send you anywhere that they feel is suitable for your age and abilities – a state, public or private school – or they can educate you at home.

Home education

The law allows your parents to educate you at home, as long as they provide you with an efficient and suitable education. They can do this themselves or provide you with a home teacher. In order to do this they have to inform your local education authority (LEA), or the Department of Education in Northern Ireland. The LEA then has to make sure your home education is meeting the right requirements. If they feel it isn't then your parents could face legal action.

If your parents withdraw you from school, they must inform the school and the LEA and make sure you are no longer registered at school. If they do not do this, action will be taken for non-attendance.

Being too ill to go to school

The 1996 Education Act also states that the LEA has to provide some kind of education for pupils who cannot attend school because of illness. However, the home tuition the LEA supplies is usually around five hours a week and not full time education.

SCHOOL ATTENDANCE

"My mum says she'll go to prison if I don't go to school. I'm sure this is just a lie to make me go, but I'm slightly worried it could be true."

Sara (13)

Under the 1996 Education Act, a School Attendance Order is served (handed to the person who has parental responsibility over you) if you are not registered at a school and not getting any education. This orders your parents to send you to school. This process will happen in the following stages:

1 A letter will be sent to your parents asking them to show the LEA you are being educated either at home or at a school.

2 If your parents don't answer, or the standard of your home education is low, another letter will be sent, saying an Attendance Order will be served and a particular school named for you. Your parents then have 15 days to agree to this school or find you another.

3 After 15 days you must be registered at a school.

4 If your parents don't do this, they will be prosecuted at a Magistrates Court and fined (they will not be put in prison).

Truanting

If you are registered at a school and don't turn up without having a valid excuse, your parents may be served with an Education Supervision Order. This is an order placed by the court on you and your parents to ensure you go to school. It's really there to help you sort out any problems you may be having and is supervised by an education welfare officer who will work with you and your parents.

The welfare officer will investigate your case, and start by visiting your parents. He or she will then visit you, and try to find out why you won't attend school. If there is no real reason why you won't go, and you still refuse to attend, the supervision order will be served.

If you still don't go to school, and/or you are thought to be beyond parental control, Social Services may seek a Care Order in relation to you, though this is usually a last resort. Care Orders place you in the care of the Social Services, and they will now share responsibility for you with your parents.

NATIONAL CURRICULUM

The National Curriculum is the name given for all the subjects and topics you are required to study in a state school. These subjects are considered to be a basic education and are: maths, English, science, a foreign language, technology, music, art, physical education and history and geography (though these last two subjects are not compulsory after 14).

In Scotland, as well as the National Curriculum, religious education, PE and Gaelic in Gaelic speaking areas are also compulsory. However, your parents can withdraw you from religious education lessons.

SCHOOL UNIFORM

It is up to your school to decide whether or not you have to wear a school uniform. They also have the right to say you can't wear jewellery or tattoos or have body piercing. If you don't stick to the rules, you will be subject to disciplinary actions from the school.

SCHOOL REPORTS

All state schools will keep reports on you. These reports will contain your academic records, your behaviour in school, your attendance record and any other information from teachers.

- If you are under 16 you have no right to see this report, but your parents can request a copy.
- If you're over 16, you are entitled to see a copy.
- If you are 18, you are entitled to see a copy and exclude your parents from seeing it.

DISCIPLINE AT SCHOOL

Just because you are required to go to school, it doesn't mean your rights disappear when you walk through the school gates. However, your school has a right to lay down codes of behaviour expected from you within school hours and when you are on school grounds. They can also punish you if you break these rules.

Possible Punishments

- Being sent home from school for the day. (Usually a punishment for some kind of disruptive behaviour or uniform problem.)
- Being held in detention.
  If you get put in detention, your parents should be notified, so they know where you are.

Corporal Punishment

Corporal Punishment is any kind of assault on you by a teacher for the breaking of rules or disruptive behaviour. It includes slapping, hitting, kicking, shaking, pulling of hair or ears, and the throwing of objects like a book or chalk rubber.

Corporal punishment has been unlawful in state schools since 1987 and now cannot be used in any school.

RESTRAINING A PUPIL

There is an exception to the above rule. Teachers can use reasonable force if it's needed to control or restrain a pupil to stop someone from getting hurt. For example, teachers have the right to:

- physically intervene if another pupil is being attacked
- prevent a pupil from committing a criminal offence
- prevent a pupil from injuring themselves
- prevent a pupil from injuring others
- prevent a pupil from being overly disruptive and/ or inciting the behaviour of others
- defend themselves against an attack

They can use any of the following means to do this:

- holding
- pushing
- pulling
- shepherding a pupil away, by placing a hand at the small of their back
- using a restrictive hold in extreme circumstances

However, these methods are not methods of punishment and cannot be used this way. They are only methods of restraint.

What to do if a teacher uses corporal punishment on you for no reason

If a teacher goes beyond reasonable force or punishes you severely for no reason, he/she may be guilty of assault, which you should first report to your parents, and then the police, your local education authority and your headteacher.

Being excluded or expelled from school

What the words mean

expelled/permanently excluded thrown out of a school and not allowed to return

excluded not allowed at school for a certain period of time

"My headteacher says my hair is too long and I have to get it cut or she'll expel me. Can she really make me have my hair cut?"

Mike (14)

Expulsion or exclusion usually happens when a school sees a pupil's behaviour as disruptive, violent and/or unacceptable. As you can see these terms are very loose and often, what's acceptable at one school proves to be unacceptable at another. Pupils have been excluded for all kinds of different reasons, from having a nose ring to something more disruptive.

The final decision about whether you are excluded or expelled over something comes down to your head-teacher.

What's more, unlike in other areas of the law, if you are under 18 you do not have the right to express your opinion on being excluded. This means you cannot get up before your teachers and plead your own case and you also have no right to express your opinion to the school's board of governors or the LEA. If you are under 18, it is also the case that no-one has to inform you personally of the decision to exclude you.

APPEALING AGAINST AN EXCLUSION

The 1996 Education Act and the School Standards and Framework Act 1998 sets out the procedure a school has to follow regarding an exclusion.

Even if your exclusion is official, you cannot be excluded for more than 15 days per term (however, you can still be permanently excluded).

Once you have been excluded, your school must inform your parents why this has happened and then they can appeal.

Appeals should first be sent to the school's governors. The next step is usually a review of the governors' decision by the LEA. There is also a further right of appeal to an independent appeal tribunal. The LEA then must consider whether the headteacher's view stands or whether you should go back to school.

EXPULSION

If you are expelled, and are under 18, whether it's from a state or private school, the LEA must still provide you with an education, either through another school or at home. A new alternative to home tuition is an off-site unit known as a Pupil Referral Unit.

SPECIAL EDUCATION NEEDS (SEN)

Special educational needs cover learning difficulties such as dyslexia, speech problems and behavioural problems. If you have one of these difficulties you are entitled to an education which helps you cope with or overcome these special needs. The 1996 Education Act says special educational need pupils should be educated within mainstream education wherever possible.

Physically disabled children have the same entitlement to state education as other children. Again, the 1996 act says disabled children should be educated wherever possible within a mainstream school.

BULLYING

> ### What the words mean
>
> **coercion** being forced to do something
>
> **intimidation** being frightened into doing something by someone
>
> **harass** to worry and annoy repeatedly

Bullying affects thousands of kids all over the UK, and while there are many organisations which offer help and advice to children who are being bullied, to their parents and to the teachers who are involved, most people still do not know what their legal rights are when they are the victim of bullying.

The Department of Education has defined bullying as the dominance of one pupil by another, or a group of others. To be seen as bullying the actions must be more than isolated incidents and must have been planned beforehand.

BULLYING can consist of...

- teasing
- name calling
- spreading gossip
- physical threats
- attacks of any kind
- being forced to do something
- intimidation
- harassment

Do schools have to stop bullying?

There is no law that says schools have to stop bullying. However, the government encourages schools to develop a policy for bullying.

They also recommend that teachers and school staff 'must act – and importantly be seen to act – firmly against bullying whenever and wherever it appears.' Schools should also:

- regularly review their policy on bullying
- seek the advice of teachers, parents and governors on a bullying policy
- make sure school prospectuses say clearly that bullying will not be tolerated
- let pupils know what to do and where to go if they are being bullied
- make sure their staff are alert to signs of bullying

If your school does not have an anti bullying policy (and remember, under law it does not have to), you should talk to your teachers or write to the school governors about starting one.

What to do if you're being bullied

The Children's Legal Centre suggests the following is the best course of action to take if you're being bullied:

INFORMAL ACTION

Tell your parents what's going on.
Write down a detailed list of what has happened to
. Make sure you note exactly what happened,
 it occurred and who was involved.

- Then with your parents, approach the school and make an complaint to your class tutor.
- Your parents should ask your teacher to investigate the bullying and take steps to protect you while at school.
- Make a note of what the teacher has said and what he/she intends to do.
- If you and/or your parents are still unhappy you should approach your headteacher, with the same information as above.
- If you and your parents are not satisfied you can take formal action.

FORMAL ACTION

- Your parents should write a letter to the school governors, explaining exactly what has happened and the action already taken. You should get a reply within 7 to 21 days.
- You can also write to the Chief Education Officer of your local education authority, however, the LEA cannot force the school to take any specific action.

LEGAL ACTION

If all else fails and/or the bullying is of a serious nature, you are within your rights to take legal action against the bullies.

Some types of bullying are seen as criminal behaviour.

- Threatening behaviour is an offence under the 1986 Public Order Act.
- Physical and sexual attacks are counted as common assault or indecent assault.

- In Scotland, if you are assaulted by a child of eight or over, it is a criminal offence and you can report the matter to the police.

When dealing with the police it's important to realise that they cannot charge a bully unless they have evidence that an incident occurred.

Bullying off school premises

Often bullying does not take place in school hours or on school grounds, making it hard for teachers to put their anti bullying policies into practice. However, teachers do have the power to discipline a pupil for misbehaviour outside school premises, and it is still worth following the actions suggested above.

BEING DISCRIMINATED AGAINST AT SCHOOL

"One of my teachers hates me. She picks on me in class and throws books at me and always gives me bad marks. Can she do this?"

Liz (14)

In all schools, state and private, you cannot be treated badly because of your sex, race, religious beliefs and/or sexuality.

For example, if you are a girl and you want to do class that is seen primarily as a boy's subject, e.g. hnical Drawing, the school cannot say no to you e grounds of your gender (because you are

If a teacher picks on you because of any of the above, then you and your parents have every right to make a complaint to your headteacher and the LEA. Remember to mark down exactly what has been said and what has occurred.

SEXUAL HARASSMENT BY TEACHERS OR OTHER PUPILS

The rules about harassment apply whatever your sex or sexuality. If you are being sexually harassed at school, by another pupil or by a teacher, tell your parents immediately.

What is Sexual Harassment?

- being touched in a sexual way
- being told sexual favours will get you higher marks
- having to listen to remarks of a sexual nature
- receiving written notes of a sexual nature

For more information about sexual harassment and what to do see the help section and p80.

Questions and answers

I've been bullied at school for nearly two years. The teachers know about it but have done nothing. What can I do because I can't bear it any longer?

Julie (14)

There is no law that says schools have to stop bullying. However, a guidance issued by the Department for Education encourages schools to develop a policy for bullying. This means teachers should do something when they see bullying going on. If your teachers are refusing to take action, you can do something by reporting the bully to your headteacher, telling your parents and considering legal action if the bullying has becoming physical.

For my 15th birthday my mum allowed me to have my hair dyed bright red. Now my head-teacher says I can't come to school until it's grown out because I have broken the school rule about dyed hair. My mum has been up loads of times to argue about it but the head won't listen. I want my say because after all this is about me. Am I allowed to do this?

Sue (15)

Unfortunately, formally you do not get a say while you are under 18. However, most schools will allow students to express their views and take those views into account. Though, if your school has a policy on pupils not having dyed hair and you have broken this, they have the right to exclude you from coming to school.

INFORMATION AND ADVICE

Education

Children's Legal Centre
University of Essex
Wivenhoe Park
Colchester
Essex CO4 3SQ
Tel: 01206 873826
(Offers free legal representation to children and parents involved in exclusion or special educational needs disputes in the S.E of England. Also produces *Bullying – A Guide To The Law.*)

Education Law Association (for specialist education lawyers)
Tel: 01293 822923

Department for Education
Great Smith Street
London SW1P 3BT
Tel: 0171 925 5000

Advisory Centre For Education
1B Aberdeen Studios
22–24 Highbury Grove
London N5 2EA
Tel: 0171 354 8321

Bullying

Anti-Bullying Campaign
10 Borough High Street
London SE1 9QQ
Tel: 0171 378 1446

Kidscape
2 Grosvenor Gardens
London SW1W ODH
Tel: 0171 730 3300

Discrimination

Commission For Racial Equality
Elliot House
10–12 Allington Street
London SW1E 5EH
Tel: 0171 828 7022

CHAPTER THREE

Your Family

Families – love them or hate them, they're yours for life. However, life has a funny way of changing and sometimes, though you can't change the fundamentals – your biological mother will always be your biological mother – family set ups do change. This means you could suddenly find yourself with one parent instead of two, or living with someone new, or away from home.

As scary as this prospect is, it will rarely happen overnight or without your prior knowledge or consent. In fact, under the Children's Act 1989, children now have greater opportunities than ever before to have their wishes and views taken into account before certain legal decisions are made about their life.

So while the court may not do exactly what you want, they will listen to your views. And whether you're 17, 15 or 11, you have more rights at home than you think.

Your Family Rights

- You have the right to live in a safe environment.
- You have the right to live in a home where you are not neglected, or ill treated.
- You have the right not to be sexually, physically or emotionally abused.
- You have the right to tell a court who you want to live with if your parents are breaking up (as long as you are of an appropriate age).

PARENTAL RESPONSIBILITY

Your parents have a legal responsibility to look after you until you are 18 years old. This means they get to make decisions about your life. These include:

- what medical treatment you are to receive (up to the age of 16)
- where you live (though you may be able to make this decision yourself at 16)
- what religion you'll be
- whether you can get married before you're 18
- how to bring you up
- what kind of education you will receive
- whether/how to discipline or punish you. However, assault of any kind on anyone (no matter if you are related to them), is a criminal offence. While your parents have the right to punish you, they cannot cause you injuries or use excessive force on you.

Who's likely to have this responsibility over you?

Mothers: always have parental responsibility (as long as they don't give it up under adoption laws) as do fathers if they are married to your mother.

Fathers: If your parents aren't married, your father can only have joint parental responsibility if: (a) your mother agrees to it and (b) your father makes and is granted an application for a Parental Responsibility Order.

Adoptive Parents: If you have been adopted your adoptive parents have parental responsibility, and yo[u] birth parents do not.

Guardians: This is someone who is appointed to look after you, if your parents die. Anyone can be appointed a guardian of a child. However, it is usually a relative or someone nominated in a will by your parents.

Care Orders: If you have been placed in care, your local authority shares parental responsibility over you (see below).

Your say over parental responsibility

The courts will listen to your wishes, and feelings (but they will also take your age into consideration).

Court orders affecting where you live and who has responsibility over you

The Social Services have a duty to make sure children who are suffering or at risk of suffering are looked after. Only your local authority and the National Society for the Prevention of Cruelty to Children can apply for care and supervision orders over you.

SUPERVISION ORDER

This is where you get to live at home with your parents but you get regular visits from your social worker, to make sure you are safe.

CARE ORDER

A Care Order will place you in the care of the local ⟨So⟩cial Services which means they now share parental ⟨resp⟩onsibility with your parents over you. This means ⟨they n⟩ow have the right to make decisions about where you will live and what school you'll go to (though you have the right to be consulted). Usually you'll live at one of the following places:

- at home with your parent(s)
- the home of a suitable family friend or family member
- with a foster family
- a children's home

Just because you have been placed under a Care Order doesn't mean you can't see your friends or family. The Social Services have to make sure you receive contact UNLESS you are in danger from any of these people and it is necessary to protect you.

Your parents can ask the local authority to accomodate you if they feel they are unable to cope with you.

YOUR HOME LIFE

Abuse

You have the right to live in a safe environment and not be ill-treated. Although your parents have the right to discipline you, any kind of assault on you is a criminal offence. This includes, sexual abuse, physical abuse, mental cruelty, neglect, and abandonment.

PHYSICAL ABUSE

Though your parents are allowed to discipline you, for example by taking away your privileges or giving you a curfew, they cannot beat you, or cause you any physical injuries.

EMOTIONAL ABUSE

This is verbal abuse, being called names, taunted, bullied, picked on and deprived of affection.

NEGLECT

Not making sure you are fed and looked after. This includes not giving access to medical treatment when necessary.

ABANDONMENT

Leaving you for long periods of time on your own without proper care.

Once the Social Services have discovered what is going on (and you can contact them yourself or ask another adult to do this) they have a duty to investigate. This means a social worker will come and visit you, to assess your situation. If your parents deny them access and the Social Services feel you are in danger, they may apply for an Emergency Protection Order in relation to you. This means you can be removed from home for up to 15 days. After this time, your social worker has to decide whether or not to apply for one of the court orders listed earlier in the chapter.

LEAVING HOME

Under 16

L egally, your parents are responsible for you until you are 18 years old. However, if you choose to leave home because you are being abused, or if you are thrown out, then your local Social Services department has to make sure you are looked after somewhere else. Usually this will be a place provided by your local authority, normally a temporary foster home.

If you are unhappy at home and want to live with another relation, you can do this. (If your parents object to the person you have chosen to live with, you will need to apply for a residence order at your local court. However, the courts do not look favourably on children bringing such applications against their parents and it is in fact very rare.)

Over 16

You can also leave home at 16, with your parents' consent. If you leave home without consent, they can make an application to the High Court and try to prevent this, or contact the police, though it is rare that you will be forced to go home as long as you are not in any danger. If you have been thrown out of home, the Social Services have to house you until you are 18 years old.

Running away

If you are under 16, and you decide to run away you will put yourself in a very difficult situation as:

1 You are not legally allowed to work.
2 You cannot apply for any benefits which means you'll have no money for rent or to live on.

Even if you lied about your age, if you had nowhere to live you wouldn't have an address that a prospective employer could contact you at. All these points are reasons why you are better off seeking help closer to home. If you have a problem and can't talk to your parents, or your parents are the problem, contact one of the many help agencies at the end of this chapter.

The police also urge under 16s to try and make up with their parents and not run away. If they find an under 16 runaway, they may place him or her under police protection for 72 hours and also contact the Social Services. If you have run away the Message Home Service 0500 700 740 (24 hrs) will allow you to leave a message for your parents, to let them know you are safe.

ADOPTION

A doption was legalised in England and Wales in 1926, which means any child or young person under the age of 18 can be legally adopted in a court. Once you have been adopted your birth parents no longer have any rights over you. You are now treated as the child of your adopted family and they can change your surname to theirs, and also give you a new first name.

Anyone over the age of 21 is allowed to become an adoptive parent. But before an adoption can take place you will have to live with your adoptive parents for a trial period. After this time (if you are old enough) you will be allowed to have a say in court about how you feel regarding the adoption.

Finding your birth parents

"My friend is adopted and wants to find out more but her adoptive mum won't tell her anything. Does this mean she'll never know who her real parents are?"

Tim (14)

The 1976 Adoption Act allows adopted children to obtain their birth certificate and background file (see information for details on how to do this) when they reach the age of 18. It is this information that helps you to trace your birth parents, as it will give you your:

- original name
- your birth mother's name
- the name of the agency that placed you
- any other adoption information

DIVORCE AND SEPARATION

What the words mean

separate no longer live together as husband and wife

divorce legally end a marriage

petition an application form asking for a divorce to be granted

granted given

u nfortunately, the decision most likely to directly affect your home and family life, is your parents wanting to separate or divorce.

To get divorced one parent must start the process by filing a petition at a county court. Your parents or one of your parents then has to prove that the marriage has irretrievably broken down (in other words, that there is no chance of them getting back together).

Can anybody get a divorce?

At the time of writing this book, divorce is granted on the following grounds:

- If your parents have been apart for two years or more and they both want to be divorced.
- If one parent has had a sexual affair with another person.
- If they have been apart for five years or more (even if one parent objects to the divorce).

- If one parent has behaved unreasonably, for example been abusive, or has a problem with drugs or gambling.
- If one parent has deserted the family for two years or more.

In N. Ireland there is only one ground for divorce – the irretrievable breakdown of marriage. What's more a person cannot start divorce proceedings until they have been married for at least two years.

Who will you live with?

"My parents are separating. I have to decide who I want to live with. I don't know what to do. Will anyone really listen to me?"

Sophie (13)

After a petition is filed, your parents will begin to discuss all their joint affairs. This can be done through a family mediation counsellor, and the big topic will usually be your welfare and who you get to live with.

The 1989 Children's Act now allows all children and young people of sufficient maturity to have a say in who they want to live with and why. This is usually done through a court welfare officer. However, you can ask to speak to the judge in charge of the case (though not all will agree to this). The court will then act in your best interests by taking your happiness and wishes into account before making a decision. The older you are the more likely you are to get to live with who you want. Once a decision has been made, the Court can make the following orders:

RESIDENCE ORDER

Under this order, the court says who you will live with after a divorce. This usually happens when your parents can't agree. Some orders will divide your time between both parents, others will place you with one parent (usually the one you are already living with). Sometimes, this residence order can be given to another adult or relative, who will then also have parental responsibility in relation to you.

CONTACT ORDERS

This order is all about seeing the parent you're not living with. It says it's fine for you to stay overnight with the parent you're not living with, as well as maintain regular contact with him/her.

SPECIFIC ISSUE ORDER

If your parents cannot agree on one area of your life, they can petition for a specific issue order. This usually happens after a divorce and is often to do with moving abroad and/or education issues.

The main part of this order is called 'prohibited (forbidden) steps'. This means one parent is not allowed to do something another parent is against. For example, move with you to America or send you to boarding school.

'Divorcing' your parents

You might have heard in the news about children 'divorcing' their parents. But before you get excited, this isn't exactly right. Under the law children cannot divorce their parents; divorce can only occur between two people who are married to each other. However, you can ask to live away from your parents if you cannot get on together, or they have not been looking after you. If your relationship with your parents has completely broken down and/or you are completely unhappy at home, the Social Services may apply for a Prohibited Steps or a Specific Issues Order. They will only seek a Care Order if you are at risk of suffering significant harm.

Step families

"Apart from my real mum and dad and my sister, I have a step mum, a half sister and three step brothers. Now my mum is marrying again and soon I will have a stepsister and two more step brothers. Sometimes, I get really confused about who's part of my family."

Rebecca (13)

What the words mean

step parent If either of your parents chooses to marry again, a step parent is another name for their new spouse (wife or husband) in relation to you.

step brothers and **step sisters** These are the children from your step parent's first marriage/relationship. They are only related to you by law, not by biology or blood.

half brothers and **half sisters** These are the children your parents have with other people. You are related to them by law and by blood.

Even if your parent remarries, your step parent does not have parental responsibility for you. However, if you are in their care, they do have to look after your welfare. A step parent can also be appointed to act as your guardian (if your parent dies) and if they then divorce your parent, they can apply for a contact order, so you can still see them.

YOUR NAME

The law states that all babies should be registered with a name within six weeks of birth. However, registration is just a record and doesn't mean you have to keep that name for the rest of your life.

Despite the fact most children are given their father's surname, there is no law requiring this, which is why some children have their mother's surname. If you or one of your parents did want to change your surname, you would need the consent of both parents (even if they are unmarried or divorced).

Your first name is a matter of choice, simply because no-one can make you call yourself anything, not even your family (though, legally you can never alter a name on a birth certificate). You can change it at any age by simply using a different name.

However, written evidence is often needed of a change of name for official reasons like passports and you have to be at least 16 before you can give what is known as a public notice that you will be changing your name. This can be done by:

- changing your name by deed poll at the High Court
- putting an advert in the local paper
- signing what is known as a statutory declaration

YOUR MARRIAGE

You can get married when you are 16 with your parent's consent (and without it in Scotland) and at 18 without your parent's consent. While you can marry your cousin, it is against the law to marry a grandparent or step parent, and for a girl to marry her brother or uncle, and a boy to marry his sister or aunt.

> "My friend is in love with her step brother. I didn't think this was allowed."
>
> Chrissie (14)

There is no law against marrying your step brother if you are a girl, or your step sister if you are a boy. However it is illegal to marry a half brother or half sister.

YOUR RELIGION

You can decide to follow any or no religion. Even if you choose a different religion to your parents there is little they can do about it. However, you cannot join a sect or cult that could be harmful to you, if you are under 18. If you do and your parents object they can make you a ward of court.

Questions and answers

I want to leave home and live with friends. My mum says no way, and that she can make me stay at home until I am 18 years old. But my friends say I can leave at 16 – who's right?

Mark (15)

Essentially your mum is right. You need parental consent to leave home before the age of 18 years. However, if you leave without consent, it's unlikely the police would force you to go home again. Your parents could, however, take a High Court order out on you to stop you from leaving, though this is unlikely to be granted unless you were putting yourself in danger.

If you are planning on leaving home without consent, it's worth remembering that you are only entitled to reduced benefit until you're 18 years old, and that you cannot work full time until you have officially left school.

I read somewhere that you can get married at 15 without your parent's consent if you did it in a country where it is legal. Is this true?

Gill (15)

No, it is illegal to get married without consent anywhere in the world before the age of 16 if you usually live in England, Wales or N. Ireland. Any marriages performed before this age are invalid and not recognised by your law. If you are English, even if you go to a country where under 16s can legally get married, the marriage is not recognised in your country. If you are 16 and want to get married here, you need to have written consent from your parents.

INFORMATION AND ADVICE

If you need help, contact one of the following organisations:

Childline 0800 1111
24 hour freephone helpline for children and young people.

Careline 0181 514 1177
Confidential counselling service for young people.

National Society for the Prevention of Cruelty to Children (NSPCC)
Helpline 0800 800 500

NCH Action For Children
85 Highbury Park
London N5 1UD
Tel: 0171 226 2033

Parent Network
44–46 Caversham Road
London NW5 2DS
Tel: 0171 485 8535
Provides Parent-Link support groups for parents and
children who need help.

Family issues

National Family Mediation
9 Tavistock Place
London WC1H 9SN
Tel: 0171 383 5993

**National Organisation for Counselling Adoptees
and their Parents
(NORCAP)**
3 New High Street
Headington
Oxford OX3 7AJ
Advice line 01865 750554

Post Adoption Centre
Torriano Mews
Torriano Avenue
London NW5 2SG
Tel: 0171 284 0555

**British Agencies for Adoption and Fostering
(BAAF)**
11 Southwark Mews
London SE1 1RQ
Tel: 0171 593 2000

For your birth certificate write or phone for an information pack:

Adoption Section
General Register
Trafalgar Road
Southport PR8 2HH
Tel: 01704 563563

Advice, Advocacy and Representation for Children in Care (ASC)
1 Sickle Street
Manchester M60 2AA
0800 616101

Who Cares Trust? (for people in care)
Kemp House
152–160 City Road
London EC1V 2NP
Tel: 0171 251 3117

Shelter
88 Old Street
London EC1V 9HU
Tel: 0171 253 0202

National Missing Person's Helpline
0500 700 700 (24 hrs)

Message Home Service
0500 700 740 (24 hrs)
Message service for runaways.

National Stepfamily Association
Chapel House
18 Hatton Place
London EC1N 8RU
Tel: 0990 168 388

National Council For One Parent Families
255 Kentish Town Road
London NW5 2LX
Tel: 0171 267 1361

Families Need Fathers
134 Curtain Road
London EC2A 3AR
Tel: 0181 886 0970

Network of Access and Child Contact Centres
St Andrew's with Castlegate
URC
Goldsmith Street
Nottingham NG1 5JT
Tel: 0115 948 4557

The Children's Legal Centre publish a guide *Working
with Young People* which is available from them (see
p143 for address).

CHAPTER FOUR

Your Sex Life

Sex is private, right? Having sex is your own choice, right?

Well, if you're under 16, this whole subject isn't so private. This is because the law sees girls under 16 as being in need of protection. This means a boy who has sex with a fifteen-year-old girl could be prosecuted. It also means that seeking contraception isn't so simple. What's more, learning about sex isn't as easy as opening a book, and discovering it all and sex education in school often has huge gaps within it. Gaps that could mean some of you will lose out on discovering what your sexual rights actually are.

Your Sexual Rights

- You have the right to say no to sex.
- You have the right to sex education and information.
- You have the right to get married at 16 with parental consent.
- You have the right to choose your own sexual partner.

THE AGE OF CONSENT

What the words mean

age of consent the age when it is legal for you to agree to have sex

underage sex sex before you reach the age of consent

Girls cannot legally have sex until they are 16 years old, or 17 in N. Ireland. However, if a girl under 16 does have sex and this is discovered, it's the boy and not the girl who can be prosecuted. This is because he is the one committing a criminal offence, not her.

If the couple are the same age or the boy a year or so older than the girl, it is unlikely a prosecution would take place. But if the man happened to be a lot older than the girl he could receive a prison sentence.

The age of consent for homosexuals used to be 21 years old, but it is now 18 years old, and the law is currently being looked at, as many people believe homosexual sex should be legal at 16, too. Lesbians are not covered by the law.

CONTRACEPTION

What the words mean

confidentiality This means the person who you tell information to should not tell anyone else what you have said. If he/she intends to do so, they should tell you so before you give them any information. (See also chapter 1.)

You have the right to consult any doctor for contraception and know that whatever you say will be kept between you and him/her. Even if a doctor says no to what you want he/she cannot tell your parents why you have come to see him, unless it is an emergency situation.

However, bear in mind that the doctors will undoubtedly try to persuade you to tell your parents.

When confidentiality can be broken

There are two areas where professionals feel breaking confidentiality is justified.

- Where you are at risk of suffering harm.
- Where your life or that of another person is at risk.

The legal position on contraception

The law regarding under 16s and contraception basically says it is up to a doctor to decide if an under 16 asking for contraception is mature enough to understand what they are doing. If he/she thinks they are he can give them contraception. The British Medical Association also says if a doctor acts in good faith to protect a girl against the potentially harmful effects of intercourse, he would not be acting illegally.

This basically means doctors have the right to judge whether or not they think you're mature enough to receive contraception before they give it to you. A doctor will judge this on your ability to understand the choices he or she is offering you and your reasons behind wanting contraception.

In practice, young people who want to protect themselves against an unplanned pregnancy and disease are generally likely to be considered competent from the age of 13. Most doctors think if you're adult enough to ask for contraception, you're adult enough to be given it. Their prime concern is not to give you a lecture on the perils of underage sex but to prevent an unwanted pregnancy or a sexual disease.

Even if your doctor considers you to be too immature he/she has to keep your request confidential and you are still free to go to another doctor or clinic and ask again. Doctors may encourage you to tell your parents; however, they cannot force you to. If you are at all worried about visiting your family GP, visit a Brook Advisory Centre instead. They specialise in counselling and advising young people on contraception and sex.

How easy is it to get contraception and advice?

"Is it true I can ask for contraceptive advice and go into a shop and buy a condom if I'm under 16?"

Mark (14)

It's easier than you may think. It may be against the law for a boy to have sex with a girl under 16 but it is not illegal for anyone to use or buy contraceptives if they are under 16. Condoms are readily available from chemists, supermarkets and even some record stores, and they are also free at Family Planning and Brook Advisory Clinics. It's also not illegal to seek contraceptive advice. This is readily available from places like Brook Advisory Centres and the Family Planning Association. Information and advice concerning contraception also forms a part of sex education in schools.

Where to go if you don't want to see your GP

BROOK ADVISORY CENTRES

Brook Advisory Centres were founded in London in 1964 in response to the fact that unmarried people who wanted contraceptive advice and information had nowhere to go. In 1967 the NHS (Family Planning) Act permitted local authorities to give contraceptive advice to the unmarried for the first time and Brook pledged to see under 16s. However it wasn't until 1974 that contraception became free to everyone.

Brook now offers young people free, confidential birth control advice and can also help with emotional and sexual problems. No matter what your reason for going to Brook, everything you discuss will be private and confidential. Even if your worries have nothing to do with contraception and you need to talk about a relationship or your sexual feelings this is the place to go. So if you need immediate information about contraception, pregnancy testing, abortion, sexually transmitted diseases or emergency after sex contraception this is the place for you. For more information contact *Brook Advisory Centres* 0171 713 9000.

FAMILY PLANNING CLINICS

Family planning is free to everyone on the National Health Service. The Family Planning Association provides a national information and advice service on contraception, safer sex and reproductive health care. They also have details of where your local clinics are though they do not run the local clinics. You can call them on 0171 636 7866 between 9am and 5pm for details. If you want to find your nearest family planning doctor or clinic you can also look in your local directory or your local library. Most chemists can also provide this information. Some family planning clinics also run special young people's sessions. Again, everything that goes on at these clinics is completely confidential.

UNPLANNED PREGNANCY

Every year, 200,000 women in Britain find themselves with an unplanned pregnancy. Free pregnancy tests can be done at your GP's, a family planning clinic or a Brook Advisory Centre. You can also buy a pregnancy testing kit at any chemist at any age.

Your options if you have an unplanned pregnancy

• KEEPING THE BABY

No one can make you give up a child you want, even if you are under 16 as long as you show you are competent and capable of looking after a child.

• ABORTION

Abortions have been legal in England, Wales and Scotland since the 1967 Abortion Act but they are not available on request. In order to get an abortion, two doctors must agree that you have 'grounds' i.e. a good reason for an abortion. If you want an abortion on the NHS, one of those doctors would generally be your GP and the other the doctor at the local hospital who would be in charge of the actual abortion.

To have an abortion you need to be less than 24 weeks pregnant (though very few doctors now perform an abortion after 20 weeks) and have your doctors agree that:

- Your mental or physical health is at risk or
- There is a risk that the baby would be born suffering from a physical or mental abnormality that would make it seriously handicapped.

If you don't want to see your GP and/or he/she is against abortion then you can go to any pregnancy advisory service, where they will help and advise you. However, you will have to pay in excess of £250 for an abortion, and the doctors still have to adhere to the above.

In N. Ireland, the 1967 Abortion Act does not apply. Abortions are only performed when there is a serious risk to health or life.

Age and abortion
Once a girl is 16 years old she can legally decide to have an abortion without asking for her parent's consent.

If you are under 16 years old it is very unlikely that a doctor will agree to do an abortion without parental consent. If you want an abortion and your parents don't want you to have one, then you can ask a social worker to help you. If an agreement cannot be reached, a court will have to decide the matter.

If you are under 18 (classified as a young person in the eyes of the law), your parents can try to stop you from having an abortion by making an application to the High Court, however the court will listen to what you have to say.

It is important to know that an abortion cannot be done against your wishes even if you are under 16.

• ADOPTION (see also chapter 3)

If you choose to put a child up for adoption, then you need to get in touch with the Adoption and Fostering section of your local Social Services department (number in phone book). Couples are selected very carefully to make sure they will make good parents so your child has every chance of going to a good home.

• FOSTERING

You may find you want to look after your baby but are having problems with housing or money. In this case it may be possible to have your baby fostered for a while. This means placing your child temporarily with a family selected by the Social Services.

SEX EDUCATION

"Our sex education lessons are so embarrassing. Our Geography teacher has to do them and he goes bright red and mumbles the minute he has to explain anything. The boys are really horrid to him and ask him really stupid questions so he'll go red. Do I have to go?"

Helen (14)

What you're entitled to

Since August 1994 ...

- Sex education is compulsory, including information about HIV/AIDS and other sexually transmitted diseases, in all secondary schools.
- Parents have the right to withdraw their children from all or part of the sex education lessons which are not part of the National Curriculum.

This means your parents have no say over what you can and can't learn under the National Curriculum, so they cannot stop you from learning about the scientific aspects of sex – how babies grow. However, some aspects of sex education which are now taught in all secondary schools, particularly the non biological aspects of sex, such as how to handle relationships or sexual orientation, are not under the National Curriculum. This means your parents can stop you from receiving those lessons – so you could miss out on vital information on topics such as sexually transmitted diseases, contraception, and gay and lesbian issues.

In N. Ireland teachers are told that sex education should fit in with the moral and religious principles held by parents and the school.

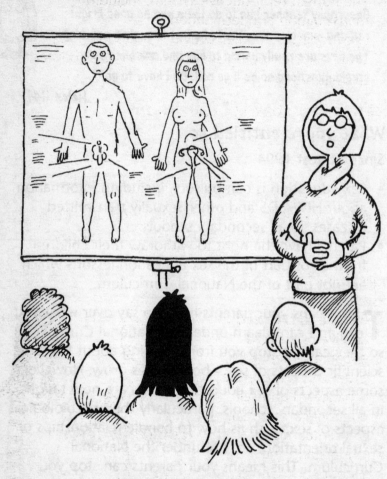

COMPULSORY SEX EDUCATION in England, Wales and N. Ireland (National Curriculum science)

Scottish schools are expected to have a sexual health programme based on guidelines from the Scottish Office.

Key Stage 3
- The physical and emotional changes that take place during adolescence.
- The human reproductive system, including menstruation and fertilisation.
- Life processes and cell activity – ways in which some cells, including sperm and ova, are adapted to their functions.

NOT COMPULSORY SEX EDUCATION

Key Stage 2
- Begin to know about and have some understanding of the physical, emotional and social changes which take place at puberty.
- Know the basic biology of human reproduction and understand some of the skills necessary for parenting.

Key Stage 3
Psychological aspects
- Be able to give and receive praise and encouragement in order to promote the self esteem and self confidence essential to mental health.

- Understand the emotional changes which take place during puberty.
- Understand differences in maturation and have a positive self image.

What if your parent withdraws you from sex education?

If your parent withdraws you from sex education your teachers cannot give you advice on any sexual matter without your parent's consent. However, a teacher can tell you where to seek confidential help (e.g. at a local clinic or with your GP) as this is not seen as providing sex education but merely giving you information as to where you can legally get advice. These organisations will happily give you any information you need.

SEXUAL OFFENCES

Rape

This is defined as sexual intercourse without consent. It occurs when a man forces someone to have penetrative sex (with the penis) when they do not want to. Getting someone drunk or drugging them in order to have sex both count as rape.

Under the law a woman cannot rape a man though it can be counted as indecent assault. (See the glossary at the back of the book for a definition of this and other sexual offences.)

Being a victim of an assault

If you are the victim of any type of sexual assault you have the right to report it to the police, and seek confidential help and advice.

In the case of rape, the police ask victims to avoid washing and changing their clothes until they have been examined. This is so that vital evidence like semen and blood can be taken as evidence.

In a rape unit you will be examined by a female doctor, and talked to by a female officer. Later you will have to go to court and give evidence as a witness.

All victims of sexual offences are treated specially in court. For a start your name is never revealed, and secondly you can give evidence from behind a screen so you don't have to look at the person who attacked you.

Those under the age of 17 can even give their testimony by a video recording, and only appear to be cross examined by the defence team.

Questions and answers

I'm 14 years old. If I ask for the pill and my doctor says no, does this mean he can tell my parents what I came in for?

Vicki (14)

You have the right to consult any doctor for contraceptive advice at any time you want because this is not breaking the law. You also have the right to confidentiality with your doctor, which means whatever you say should be kept between you and him.

Even if a doctor will not prescribe you contraception, he/she cannot tell your parents why you have come to see him. However, bear in mind that the doctor will undoubtedly try to persuade you to tell your parents – but cannot tell them behind your back unless it is an emergency situation. He also cannot force you to tell your parents.

My boyfriend is 14 and I am 16 and we want to have sex. My best friend says it's illegal because he's only 14. So if we have sex, I will be breaking the law but his friend says it would only be illegal, if I was under 16. Who's right?

Tina (16)

Your boyfriend's friend is right. The age of consent only applies to girls. This means if a man has sex with a girl who is under this age, he will be committing a criminal offence, even if she said yes. However, if a woman has sex with a boy under 16, she is not committing an offence, unless the boy was forced into it, or the age difference was very large (e.g. 13 and 30 years). In that case, the woman could be charged with indecent assault.

INFORMATION AND ADVICE

Brook Advisory Centres
Tel: 0171 713 9000
(for details of your nearest clinic)

Family Planning Association
27–35 Mortimer Street
London W1N 7RJ
Tel: 0171 636 7866
(for details of your nearest clinic)

Marie Stopes International
Marie Stopes House
108 Whitfield Street
London W1P 6BE.
Tel: 0171 388 2585

Pregnancy Advisory Service
11–13 Charlotte Street
London W1P 1HD.
Tel: 0171 637 8962

British Pregnancy Advisory Service
Austy Manor
Wootton Wawen
Solihull
West Midlands B95 6BX
Tel: 0564 793225

National Aids Helpline
0800 567123 (24 hours)

The Children's Legal Centre publish a full guide to
Confidentiality which is available from them (see p143
for address).

CHAPTER FIVE

Your Work

Working on a daily basis is tough, and working while being at school is even tougher. This is why the whole area of work and under 18s is very strictly regulated. No-one wants to go back to the days of child labour, when children as young as five years old were forced to work in factories for very little money. What's more, no-one wants to see adults or children working in dangerous conditions, where their health and lives are put at risk. This is why rules and regulations on the work front have to be stuck to. Don't put yourself at risk, know your rights, obey the laws and protect yourself.

Your Work Rights

- You can take certain part time jobs when you are 13 years old.
- Once you have left full time education at 16 years old, you can legally take a full time job.
- You have the right to make a complaint about an employer if s/he is harassing you, making you do dangerous work and/or making you do long hours.
- You have the right to work in a safe environment.

PART TIME WORK WHEN UNDER 16

Jobs on which there are no age restrictions

 "I've heard you have to be 16 to get a job in a shop, but is it OK to wash cars and baby-sit before I get to that age?"
Suzanne (14)

As long as the person giving you the job isn't running a business you are allowed to do the following jobs and get paid for them, provided you do them out of school hours.

- baby-sitting – though if you're below 13 years, it's unlikely you will be employed as a baby-sitter. The NSPCC recommends that all baby-sitters should be aged at least 16 to ensure that the children being looked after are properly protected.
- cleaning cars
- odd jobs such as errands or gardening

Other jobs

You can take other part time jobs once you are 13 years old, however, there are a number of restrictions on the hours you can work (paid or unpaid), when you can work and where you can work. These restrictions are in place to ensure that you are not exploited.

Even if your family runs a business such as a shop or a restaurant they cannot make you work all the time. No matter whether you are related to them or not, you are still subject to the same work restrictions as any other 13 years old. These are:

- You cannot work before 7am or after 7pm.
- You cannot be forced to do work for your family.
- You can only work for 2 hours or less each day.
- You cannot work as a street trader – this includes selling newspapers, flowers, or working on a market stall.
- You cannot work on a night shift.
- You cannot go busking.
- You cannot do a job where heavy lifting, carrying or working on industrial equipment is required.

"I used to work in a place down the road that employed kids under 16 to work in the stockroom, carrying boxes. I stopped going when one of my friends broke his leg when a box fell on him."

Baz (15)

- You cannot drive or ride in an agricultural tractor or machine.
- You cannot work on board any ship.
- You cannot work in a factory or any industrial place.
- You cannot work on a building site.
- You cannot work on any kind of construction.
- You cannot work in a mine or quarry.
- You cannot work on a harbour or dock.
- You cannot work on a railway.
- You cannot work in a gas works or electricity generating station.
- You cannot work in a sewer.
- You cannot work on an inland waterway.
- You cannot work as a collector of money.
- You cannot sell scrap metal.

- You cannot work in a licensed place (somewhere that sells alcohol).
- You cannot work in a cinema, a betting shop or a kitchen.

"I want to work part time not because I want a job but because I want my own money to go out with."

Lisa (14)

What the words mean

by-laws regulations made by the local authority not the central government. They are local laws, particular to your area.

If you are thinking about taking a part time job while under 16, you should first check with your local education authority (LEA) to see what the local by-laws are. These by-laws vary from town to town. For instance in some places you will be allowed to work on a market stall if you are over 14, in other places you won't.

Your employer should also check your age and that you have parental permission to work. Many LEAs state that an employer has to register an under 16 with the education welfare department of your local education authority, if you intend to work part time. They will then give you a licence and employment card/work permit that tells you how long you can work and the work you can do in your area. An education welfare officer will then be responsible for making sure you and your employer are obeying the rules.

WHAT YOU SHOULD BE AWARE OF

If you let your school work slip, or have to take days off because you are ill from your job, the education welfare officer can make you give up your job. He can also prosecute your employer if you are working illegally. You have the right to make a complaint to the education welfare officer about any employer who is harassing you, making you do dangerous work and/or making you do long hours.

Acting and modelling

If you have been asked to perform (act) and/or model (which also counts as a performance), you must go through your local education authority and apply for a licence (see above). The local authority then has to make sure you will be looked after properly and your education will not suffer before they grant a licence. Once the licence is granted, you are covered the same way as other children working. However, the law is very strict and you are not allowed to do any of the following:

- work/performances that are considered dangerous, like acrobatics
- work/perform for more than 79 days in a 12 month period (including rehearsals)
- work/perform more than 8 hours a day
- work abroad without a special licence from a Magistrates Court

FULL TIME WORK

You cannot legally take a full time job, no matter if it's the career you intend to enter, until you have reached 16 years old. Even after you have left school you still cannot work in certain places until you are 18 years old. For example:

- An off-licence.
- Any bar during opening hours even if you are not being paid. Though you can work in the food section of a pub/bar.
- You cannot clean industrial machines.
- You cannot work in the alcohol section in a supermarket.
- You cannot work at a betting shop.

WHAT'S EXPECTED OF YOU WHEN YOU START WORK

Everyone who takes on a job agrees to a contract of employment with their employer. This means you agree to do work for a certain amount of wages and your boss agrees to pay you for your work. A contract of employment also means that you must do your job to a reasonable standard, obey work rules (these should be reasonable) and be honest. Your employer must make sure your work environment is safe and healthy and pay your wages (these should be agreed before you start work).

PROTECTING YOURSELF

Before you start work, you can protect yourself by knowing the following:

- What you will be paid (there is no minimum wage for under 21s. This means employers can pay you what they want and it is up to you to decide whether to accept or not).
- What happens when you're sick and what (if anything) you are entitled to.
- What happens if you are injured at work.
- What to do if you have a complaint.
- What notice (time between announcing you are quitting your job and leaving) is required on either side.
- The hours you are expected to work.
- Any conduct (how you're supposed to behave) issues.

UNFAIR DISMISSAL

Unfortunately if your boss sacks you unfairly there is very little you can do. Only people who have worked for the same employer for 2 years or more and for more than 16 hours a week, can bring an unfair dismissal claim.

YOUTH TRAINING

Even though you can leave school at 16, you are excluded from benefits until you are 18. This means 16 and 17 year olds not in full time education can only get reduced income support for being unemployed. Instead the government will place you on a Youth Training (YT) programme. There is no guarantee of a job at the end of a YT programme.

The Youth Training schemes are government funded and most people are recruited through career offices. Just like any other job, you have certain rights when working on a YT scheme, though because you are considered a trainee, rather than an employee, you do not have the full rights of someone in a full time job.

SAFETY

The Health and Safety at Work Act 1974, says it is up to your employer to make sure the workplace is safe. Therefore, he or she has to ensure the following:

• The areas in which you work are safe.
• Equipment you work with must be safe.

- You are working with people who are competent and don't put your safety at risk.
- You are properly supervised.
- You receive proper training so that you don't injure yourself at work.

DISCRIMINATION

The law is very strict on the area of discrimination (the Sex Discrimination Act 1975 and Race Relations Act 1976 cover these areas). You cannot be judged by your sex, race, marital status, religious beliefs and/or sexuality. These laws apply to you whatever your age and whatever kind of work you do.

Areas covered by these laws:

- You cannot be denied a job on these grounds.
- You cannot be treated unfairly on these grounds.
- You cannot be denied training courses other people have been sent on, on these grounds.
- You cannot be denied promotion on these grounds.
- Jobs cannot be labelled by race, unless it is a direct qualification for the job.
- Jobs cannot be labelled by gender or marital status.
- Since the Equal Pay Act of 1975, it has been illegal to pay men and women differently for doing the same job. New regulations in 1984 mean women can now compare their earnings with men's in a different but equally valuable job.

SEXUAL HARASSMENT

What the words mean

Industrial Tribunal an independent board not linked to the courts which hears complaints about sexual harassment and unfair dismissal

The rules about harassment apply whatever your sex or sexuality. If you are being sexually harassed by a workmate always remember to make a complaint in writing and keep a copy for yourself. If it is your boss, tell your parents and think about reporting him to an Industrial Tribunal (details of how to do this are available from your local job centre).

If you're not sure exactly what sexual harassment is, see p41.

Who's to blame for sexual harassment?

Sexual harassment has a lasting effect on the victim and years later many people still admit how defeated they feel by events that took place years ago. If you are being harassed then you need to tell someone what's going on as soon as possible. If you feel weak and helpless by what's happening to you remember:

- Sexual harassment has been proven to ruin self-confidence.
- You are not to blame for what is happening. You are the innocent victim.
- People who sexually harass thrive on their victims' silence.
- If someone doesn't believe you are being harassed, you must keep on telling, until someone believes you.

Informal action

- Tell your parents what's going on.
- Write down a detailed list of what has happened to you. Make sure you note exactly what happened, when it occurred and who was involved.
- Then with your parents, approach your employer and ask him or her to take action.

Legal action

If that fails, you are within your rights to take legal action against the person harassing you.

- Threatening behaviour is an offence under the 1986 Public Order Act.
- Physical and sexual attacks are counted as common assault or indecent assault. Contact the police with details of the harassment you have suffered.

TAX

Near your 16th birthday you will automatically be sent a National Insurance Number. When you start a job you will have to give this number to your employer, so that NI payments can be deducted from your wages (those on a YT scheme do not have to pay NI contributions). These contributions are compulsory and have to be paid on full time and part time work. NI contributions go towards paying you benefits if you are ill, have a baby, injured or become unemployed.

BANK ACCOUNTS

You can open a bank account from the age of seven, pay money in and draw it out yourself. However, the bank probably won't give you a current account with a chequebook and a cheque guarantee card until you are 18 years old, able to work full time and have a monthly salary coming into your account.

You also cannot get a credit card (unless your parent agrees to pay your debts should you get into trouble) and you cannot apply for loans if you are under 18.

Questions and answers

My parents run a shop and make me work in it after school and on the weekends. They don't pay me so they say it's OK for me to do it. I'm only 12 and I think this is really unfair. Can they do this?

Dawn (12)

Work regulations for under 16s are very strict. For a start you have to be aged 13 or over to work for someone whether it is paid or not. Even if you're 13 years old, you cannot work before 7am or after 7pm. You cannot be forced to do work for your family and you can only work for two hours or less each day. Even if your family runs a business such as a shop or a restaurant etc. they cannot make you work all the time. No matter whether you are related to them or not, you are still subject to the same work restrictions as any other child.

My sister's workmate is always trying to kiss her and touch her. I told her she should tell our mum, but she says this man will make trouble for her if she does that. Can he get away with doing this?

Fran (14)

No-one, no matter who they are, has the right to sexually harass anyone. Your sister has a number of rights, including reporting this man to an industrial tribunal, reporting him to their boss and/or reporting him to the police. She should keep note of all the things this man has said and done to her, as evidence against him.

INFORMATION AND ADVICE

Working

Department of Employment
Caxton House
Tothill Street,
London SW1H 9NF
Tel: 0171 273 3000.

Discrimination

Commission For Racial Equality
Elliot House
10-12 Allington Street
London SW1E 5EH
Tel: 0171 828 7022

Rights of Women
52-54 Featherstone Street
London EC1Y 8RT
Tel: 0171 251 6577

CHAPTER SIX

You and the Police

Having to deal with the police, the courts and the criminal justice system is scary and confusing at any age. What's more, thanks to an overabundance of TV cop shows, most of us now think the police are either out to get us or completely incompetent.

The fact is, they are simply here to keep the peace and enforce the law. Without them, there would be no-one to turn to when you were in trouble and needed help, and no-one to intervene when someone was committing an offence against you. If you still think the police force are a waste of time, imagine a world without them. Who would you turn to for help if someone robbed you? Who would you ask to step in if someone threatened a member of your family? And who would uphold all the laws that make our daily lives safe and secure?

This doesn't mean, however, that they have the right to do whatever they want whenever they want. The police and the courts have to stick to the law like any other organisation, and this means they have to respect your rights at all times.

Your Legal Rights

- You have the right to be protected from criminal activity.
- You have the right to approach the police for help.
- You have the right to ask for legal representation in a police station.
- You have the right to ask for your parents to be present in a police station.

AGE AND CRIME

Age is an important factor in the criminal justice system. Even though when you're under 18 you don't have the same rights as an adult in many areas in life, within the law you can be considered 'adult' in terms of understanding the implications of what is going on, from the age of 10.

The facts

UNDER 10 YEARS

If you take part in a criminal offence in England, Wales or N. Ireland when you're under this age, you are not charged simply because, in the eyes of the law, you are seen as not being able to commit a crime. This means you literally don't understand the implications of your actions. However, there have been exceptions to this law. Also, just because you are not charged, doesn't mean you'll get away scot-free. For instance, if you are causing continuous criminal damage and your parents cannot control you, the Social Services can step in (see chapter 3).

In Scotland, however, the law is different (see below).

10 – 17

You have full responsibility from the age of 10.
You are now seen as a young person, or a juvenile.
In the eyes of the law you are seen to have criminal
responsibility. This means in the eyes of the court, you
knew and understood what you were doing when you
committed a crime.

In all cases, you are subject to the law of the country
you are in, in other words, if you break the law
abroad, that is where you will be arrested and tried in
a court.

SCOTLAND

Age of Criminal Responsibility

Under 8 years
The age at which the law believes you can understand
the crime you have committed is 8 years old in

Scotland. This means you could not be prosecuted if you were under the age of eight when you committed an offence. However, you could be taken away from your parents and put in care.

8 –16 years

A Children's Panel will usually decide what will happen if you have a committed an offence. There are three options available to them:

1 To take no further action against you.
2 To grant a home supervision order. This is when the social worker will check on you at home to make sure you are coping.
3 To grant a residential supervision order whereby you will be sent to a local authority house to live and the Social Services will assume parental responsibility for you.

BEING QUESTIONED

What the words mean

loitering hanging about in a particular place for no apparent reason

"I've heard the police can stop you any time and make you answer their questions. Is this true?"

Tony (14)

The police can stop you on the street and ask you questions whenever they are worried about something, however, they can't just do it for the following reasons:

- the way you are dressed
- the colour of your skin
- because you have tattoos and/or body piercings

They have to have a good idea that you're up to something. Some reasons they might approach you are:

- If it's late at night.
- If you're hanging around with a large group of people.
- If you're loitering in one particular place.
- If alcohol is involved.
- If you are acting disruptively or aggressively.
- If you're annoying members of the public.

In N. Ireland, the laws about questioning are very complex because of the Emergency Legislation which operates here to fight terrorism. Under Emergency

Legislation, young people can be stopped and questioned and held for longer periods than in Britain, and a child as young as 10 years can be stopped and detained by the police and potentially be detained for up to seven days.

Being questioned on the street

It's tempting to be cheeky to the police, especially if you're with a group of friends, however, it's in your interests to answer correctly and politely. The ruder you are and the more lies you tell, the more the police will think you're hiding something and/or planning something. So all in all, it's better to just answer the questions and let them go on their way.

BEING SEARCHED

Unlike the American movies, the police cannot just grab you off the street, throw you up against a car and frisk you.

However, if they have just cause – for example they suspect you have something like a dangerous weapon, drugs and /or stolen goods on you – they can search you. Usually this means checking your clothes, your bags and your vehicle if you've got one. They cannot knock on your front door, walk in and search your house, without having a warrant, nor can they refuse to tell you what they are looking for. This means they have to tell you what they are doing before they attempt a search.

Intimate Searches

"Is it true that the police can just stop you and give you a body search for no reason?"

Lisa (14)

Many people are afraid the police can just give you an intimate body search whenever they want. Again this is not true. If the police decide to give you a more thorough search, they cannot do this in public and the search has to be done by an officer of the same sex as you. If you are under 14, a parent/guardian has to be contacted first.

BEING CAUTIONED

If the police then find reason to believe you are guilty of something, they will take you to the police station. Before they can talk to you further, they have to caution you. If you are under 17, this must be done in the presence of an appropriate adult (see p108).

A caution is the following: 'You do not have to say anything. But it may harm your defence if you do not mention when questioned something which you later rely on in court. Anything you do say may be given in evidence.'

AN APPROPRIATE ADULT

An appropriate adult is generally the person who has parental responsibility for you (see chapter 3). This person has to be called by the police and told that you have been arrested. They also have to be told where you have been taken and asked to be present while you are being questioned. It is their role to make sure you are treated fairly and not bullied into saying something.

Sometimes a social worker will be named as your appropriate adult. For instance:

- If you refuse to talk in front of your parent/ guardian.
- If your parent/guardian is not willing to come and be an appropriate adult.
- If your parent/guardian is involved in the crime.
- If your parent/guardian is a witness.
- If your parent/guardian is away.
- If the crime is against your parent/guardian.

People who cannot act as an appropriate adult

- a friend you name
- a solicitor

BEING ARRESTED

Being arrested means that the police have charged you with a criminal offence and you have to be kept in their custody until a court hearing has taken place.

CRIMES AND OFFENCES YOU CAN BE ARRESTED FOR:

Assault – attacking someone in some way (this area is divided into all kinds of different assaults)
Murder – killing someone
Rape – forcing someone to have sexual intercourse
Robbery – stealing
Theft – stealing from a person
Drugs – possession of or supplying a forbidden substance
Violent behaviour – acting aggressively with a weapon
Criminal damage – breaking, scratching, smashing etc. someone else's property
Driving while drunk
Threatening behaviour – disorderly conduct
Indecent exposure – exposing your genitals
Dangerous weapons – carrying illegal weapons and weapons that could do harm
Shoplifting – stealing from shops
Avoiding your fare (but only if you refuse to give your name and address)

If you commit a 'minor' offence like avoiding your fare, the police will take your name and address, and let you go home. You will be later summoned (called) to appear at a Magistrates Court.

If your crime is more serious the police will arrest you and at this stage they have to caution you again (see above). At this point a Custody Record – a record of everything that happens to you while you're at the police station – is opened. You can then do the following:

- tell someone you have been arrested
- talk to a solicitor in private. The solicitor is usually a duty solicitor – this is someone whose job is to represent people in police stations during their interviews.

After this point the solicitor will be with you all through your interview and up to your subsequent charging if the police decide they have enough evidence to take you to court.

If this happens you will be charged and released from the police station, and bailed (see below) to attend a particular court at a set time.

BAIL

This means you are allowed to leave the police station as long as you appear in court on a certain date. Bail may come with some of the following restrictions:

- You have to live at a certain address, usually your home or the home of whoever is in charge of your welfare.
- You cannot leave the country.
- You cannot have any contact with witnesses from the case.

- Your parent/guardian agrees to pay a fine if you do not turn up in court.

Bail may be refused by the court if:

- The police believe you will not turn up in court.
- The police believe you will commit another offence.
- The police believe you will injure someone.
- The police believe you will be injured.

If this happens and you are under 15, you may be placed in the care of Social Services, and be placed in secure accommodation. If you are over the age of 15 you may be placed in Social Services accommodation, if they have appropriate accommodation. Or you may be held in the remand wing of a prison.

BEING PROSECUTED

Summons

A summons is an official letter that tells you you must attend a court on a particular date and at a particular time. The summons should detail everything you need to know, like what you have been charged with, and when it occurred. If you are under the age of 18, your case will be heard in a Youth Court.

Youth Court

These courts are more informal than normal courts, and use simpler language to ensure that you understand what is going on.

Youth Courts are completely confidential and not open to the public. Decisions about what will happen if you are found guilty are taken by magistrates. These are people who are civil administrators of law (ordinary people) not Judges (trained lawyers appointed to the bench). If you are appearing at a Youth Court, you will have to go along with your appropriate adult (see p108) and your solicitor.

Like all cases in UK law, you are innocent until proven guilty – which means it's up to the prosecution to prove you have committed a crime. After you have been questioned about the charge, and witnesses heard, the magistrates will retire from the court to make their decision.

If they think the charge is not proved, you will be free to leave. If they think the charge is proved, a sentence will be passed (see p114).

Scotland

THE SHERIFF COURT

Issues such as divorce, guardianship and parental responsibilities will go to a court called the Sheriff Court. There are 49 such courts in Scotland.

CHILDREN'S PANELS

Children's panels are where ordinary people, who have been trained to understand children's problems, decide about a child's welfare. Usually under 16s are only sent to panels. Reasons for being sent may be:

- a crime
- drug abuse
- alcohol abuse
- skipping school
- being in danger at home

In front of such a panel, all under 16s get a say. So if you don't agree with why you are there say so. What's more you can appeal against any decision taken at a panel to a Sheriff (see above).

What the panel can do:

- Give you social work support.
- In difficult cases, suggest you live with a new family or in a children's home for a while.

Admitting you're guilty

If you say you're guilty of the charge, the magistrates will consider the case, your character, any previous cautions, and the fact you admitted to the offence. Then they will pass sentence.

SENTENCING

Warning This is when you will be given a verbal warning about your actions and what will happen if you commit a crime again.

Caution This is a formal warning that you are given at a police station. Unlike a warning, this will be kept on record, in case you commit another offence, when it could be referred to again in court.

Absolute discharge This happens if a court decides the matter is too small for you to be punished over.

Conditional discharge Again, the court decides not to punish you. However, if you commit another offence within three years, you will be punished for this and the last offence.

Binding Over This is a good behaviour contract that essentially says you will behave or pay a fine. The time period is usually three years.

Fine This is a sum you have to pay right away. If you are aged between 10 and 14 the sum is not more than £250. If you are aged between 14 and 18 the sum is not more than £1000. If you have hurt someone or destroyed someone's property, you can be ordered to pay them compensation money – usually up to £5000.

Attendance Orders This is where you have to attend a centre run by the police a few times a week.

Supervision Orders This places you under the supervision of a social worker. You must allow this person to visit you and assist you. If you commit another offence while under a supervision order you can be removed to a local authority home.

Probation Orders This places you under the supervision of a probation officer (probation means the suspending of sentence subject to good behaviour). The probation officer supervises your probation and makes sure you are behaving yourself.

Community Service This is a requirement that you must do unpaid community work.

Custodial Sentence
This basically means you will be deprived of your freedom for a period of time. You will not be sent to prison until you are an adult, instead you will be sent to a Young Offenders Institution.

Prison Even if you are found guilty of committing an offence, you cannot be sent to prison until you are 21 years old. A young person aged under 16 will be sent to a secure accommodation unit, and a young person aged between 16 and 21 will be sent to a Young Offenders Institution.

CRIMINAL RECORDS

What the words mean

spent used up so you don't have to declare them

convict prove to be guilty

Rehabilitation

"My brother has a criminal record. Will it follow him around for the rest of his life?"

Gina, 13

One of the most worrying things about breaking the law when you're young, is the fear that one mistake will follow you throughout your life. It is for this purpose that the Rehabilitation of Offenders Act 1974 was introduced.

Under this act, convictions can become spent. This means you have served whatever punishment the courts thought necessary, and paid your dues, so you no longer have to declare your criminal record (when you apply for a job, for example). However, certain professions such as nursing and others that involve access to vulnerable people, are exempt from this act. This means if you apply to be a nurse, you do have to declare any past convictions.

The same applies to the following professions:

solicitors	police officers
teachers	doctors
prison officers	nursery nurses
social workers	nannies

WHAT IS THE REHABILITATION PERIOD?

The length of the rehabilitation period depends on the type of sentence. It starts from the day you are convicted. If, for example, you were given a custodial sentence of six months or more, the rehabilitation period would be 5 years. This means if you were 15 when the sentence started, the conviction would be spent once you reached 20.

Fines and probations have a two and a half year rehabilitation period, and supervision orders a year. Certain criminal convictions, such as a life sentence, have no rehabilitation periods. For more information contact NACRO: National Association for the Care and Resettlement of Offenders (see the end of this chapter).

Questions and answers

My sister got caught shoplifting when she was 14 years old (she's now 18). She was given a formal caution for it. She's never done anything since and is about to start applying for jobs. Does she have to mention the shoplifting stuff?

Paula (15)

Even if your sister was given a conviction at 14 years, it's unlikely she would have to mention it now. This is because convictions can become spent. This means you are seen as having been rehabilitated and no longer have to pay for your offence by telling people about it.

I sometimes shoplift things like shampoo and lipstick, nothing very expensive. If I was ever caught, would the police just let me off with a warning because the things I lift are so small?

Sam (13)

Shoplifting is essentially just another word for stealing, therefore, the police never take it lightly. However, it is up to a shop whether or not they choose to prosecute a shoplifter. If you were caught a couple of times in the same shop, *or they had been watching you for a while, it's likely they'd take action against you. Even if they thought it was your first time, it's likely they would still call the police and inform your parents. This is because shops are keen to send a strong offputting message to people who steal.*

INFORMATION AND ADVICE

**National Association for the Care and Resettlement of Offenders
(NACRO)**
Helpline 0171 840 6464

Victim Support
National Office
Cranmer House
39 Brixton Road
London SW9 6DZ
Tel: 0171 735 9166

The Children's Legal Centre publish a guide
Working with Young People which is available from
them (see p143 for address).

CHAPTER SEVEN

Your Pleasure

It can be hard to pay attention to laws and regulations when you're out trying to have a good time. However, there are strict regulations and many rights that apply to a whole host of pleasurable activities. Why? Well, simply in order to protect you and those around you from danger and exploitation. Ignoring these rules, breaking these laws and disregarding your rights all carry tough penalties for the offender. So educate yourself about your consumer and pleasure rights, and don't let anyone take advantage of you when you're out.

SHOPPING/CONSUMER RIGHTS

Your Rights

- You have the right to expect certain standards in the goods you buy.

What the words mean

consumer the person buying

statutory rights legal rights

The Goods and Services Act, and the Sale of Goods Act, exist to protect your consumer rights. They apply to new goods, sales goods, second-hand goods, shop goods, market goods and catalogue goods. In order to be legal under these acts, the goods must be of:

- *'A satisfactory quality'* – the condition of the goods must equal their description, e.g. 'nearly new' cannot be battered and worn. This also covers the appearance and finish of the goods and their durability.
- *'Reasonably fit for their purpose'* – e.g. a raincoat must be able to keep off the rain.
- *'As described'* – this means if a shirt is labelled 100% cotton, it should not have any other material in it.

Faulty *goods*

If something you buy develops a fault (provided you didn't damage it), you have the right to a refund, in other words, your money back. You do not have to accept any of the following:

• a repair job
• an exchange
• a credit note

A shop cannot say it doesn't give refunds on faulty goods. If the seller agrees to repair the fault and it still comes back faulty, you still have a right to a refund.

The Office of Fair Trading suggests the following if there is something wrong with goods you have bought:

1 Tell the seller (shop/market trader/catalogue) as soon as possible what has gone wrong. If you cannot get back to the shop, telephone to explain the problem.
2 Take the receipt and any other proof of purchase with you when you go back to the shop.
3 If you are not satisfied with the outcome write to the shop's head office.
4 If all else fails you can sue in the small claims court. (If you are under 18, you cannot sue in your own right but must have someone, normally a parent, do it on your behalf.) This is informal and even if you lose you will not have to pay your opponent's legal costs. Forms are available from court offices. The Citizens Advice Bureau can help you with this.

You are not entitled to a refund if:

- You were told about the fault before you bought it.
- You change your mind about the product.
- You did the damage yourself.

Clothes

Likewise if you buy an item of clothing that is faulty you are entitled to a refund, even if it was in the sale (unless it had the fault clearly marked when you bought it). However, you cannot get your money back if:

- You change your mind about an item of clothing.
- The clothes don't fit.
- You no longer like the colour.

In these instances, the shop can offer you an exchange or a credit note (but they do not have to do either).

If goods are faulty you must take them back as soon as possible, to prove that the product is unusable.

Guarantees

Despite being given a manufacturer's guarantee, when you buy something your contract is still with the seller and he cannot fob you off by making you go to the manufacturer. This other guarantee is only an additional plus.

HOW TO PROTECT YOUR CONSUMER RIGHTS

1 Always keep your receipt and the bag and packaging if possible.

2 Return faulty goods as soon as possible.
3 Always deal with a manager (as they usually know about consumer rights).
4 If you get nowhere seek help at your local Citizens Advice Bureau, the Consumers Association (both free) and/or a local solicitors.

YOUR RIGHTS AT THE HAIRDRESSERS

Unfortunately, hairdressing in the UK is an unregulated industry. This means unlike in the rest of Europe, anyone can set themselves up as a hairdresser without any training whatsoever. This also means hairdressers do not have to abide by any particular laws or regulations.

This is why the National Hairdressing Council recommends people should always use state registered hairdressers. These are hairdressers who have been trained and have a certificate backed by parliament. This certificate should be on display in the salon, or in the salon window. (Call the Hairdressing Advisory Service for details of state registered hairdressers in your area.)

Though hairdressing is not covered by its own set of regulations, as a customer you are still protected by the Goods and Services Act.

This means you are entitled to a certain standard of service and so if something goes wrong, you are entitled to a refund or some sort of compensation.

However, in the case of communication breakdowns, where you end up with the wrong hairstyle or a hairstyle you don't like, you cannot claim damages. Only people with damaged hair can seek compensation.

"I went to get my hair lightly permed and it came out in really frizzy, tight curls. I was too scared to not pay the hairdresser but by the time I went back with my mum, they said it was too late for me to complain."

Sian (14)

The Hairdressing Council suggests the following advice, should your hair be damaged by a hairdresser:

• Collect evidence such as photographs and hair samples.

- Seek another hairdresser's opinion and ask them to write it down.
- If the damage is very bad, seek advice from a trichologist (hair specialist).
- If the hairdressers will not compensate you, see a solicitor and consider seeking compensation through the small claims court.
- Contact the Hairdressing Advisory Service for more advice.

Under 16s and hairdressing

Again, while there are no strict rules about under 16s and hairdressing, trained hairdressers will not perform complicated processes, like perming and colouring, without parental permission.

YOUR RIGHT TO HAVE FUN

Alcohol (see also chapter 1)

VISITING PUBS OR BARS

Once you are over the age of 14 years, you are allowed in a bar or pub. However, you cannot buy, drink or be bought alcohol on the premises. You are only allowed to be served a soft drink, in other words a non-alcoholic beverage, like a fruit juice or cola. The pub landlord is entitled to refuse to serve you alcohol if you have no proof you are over 18, and can even ask you to leave his premises.

Some pubs do have a children's certificate licence which allows children under 14 into their bars.

However, they will be restricted to a particular area, and each child has to be accompanied by an adult.

INSIDE YOUR HOME

If you are under 18, it is not illegal for you to drink at home or at someone else's home. However, a parent or adult will be committing an offence if he or she gives alcohol to a child under the age of 5. What's more if your parent sends you or any other under 18 to buy alcohol from an off-licence or supermarket, he/she will again be breaking the law.

New legislation

Recently, a government paper has recommended that the police be given new powers to tackle underage drinking. The proposal suggests that the police have the power to seize alcohol from under 18s. Under this motion under 18s found with alcoholic drinks on the street could be fined £500.

DRUGS (see also chapter 1)

If the police have reason to suspect you're carrying an illegal drug they have the right to make you turn out your pockets and bags. They can also take you to the police station and search you. If drugs are found it's likely you'll be charged with one of two offences.

Possession

This is when you are caught with an illegal drug for your own use. The police will tell your parents or guardian and inform the Social Services. It's likely that one of the following will then happen.

- You will be given a warning. This will be placed on local police files and if you offend again, this may influence the police to charge you.
- You will be given a formal caution. This is filed and kept on central police records for five years. If you offend again, it will be used against you.
- You will be charged with an offence leading to a Youth Court hearing and you may end up with a custodial sentence.

Possession with intent to supply

This is basically dealing (giving, selling and sharing drugs). This is a more serious offence and the decision to charge you with this will be based on the circumstances when you were caught and the quantity of drugs you had at that time.

RAVES

Raves, for most adults, conjure up a vision of Ecstasy induced all-night dancing, which is why there have been calls for them to be banned. While it is not an offence to go to an inside rave, the police do have the power to stop outside ones, especially if they are causing local problems.

A warning about Ecstasy
Ecstasy is the drug associated with Raves and one reason why there are now strict regulations about outside raves. Basically, Ecstasy (also known as E, MDMA and XTC) is a hallucinogenic drug that comes in tablet form. It is a Class A drug (see p17), which means it carries maximum penalties for possession (7 years and a fine) and for supply (life imprisonment and a fine).

FIREWORKS

- You cannot buy fireworks if you are under 18.
- You cannot let any fireworks off in a public place.

CINEMA/VIDEO

Films are clearly marked with film certificates, granted by the British Board of Film Censors so that it's clear which films can be seen by under 18s and which cannot.

CERTIFICATES

U – suitable for all ages.
PG – parental guidance advised (images that may disturb some children)
12 – no-one under 12 admitted (some violence)
15 – no-one under 15 admitted (some sex and violence)
18 – no-one under 18 admitted (sex, violence and disturbing images)

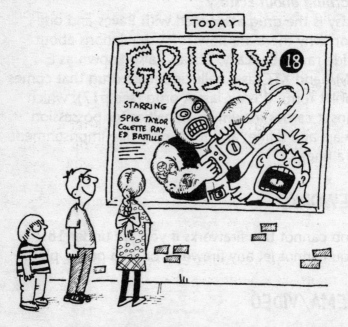

"My best friend and I are both 13 years old and last weekend the woman at the cinema wouldn't let us into a 12 certificate film. We argued for ages but she said she didn't believe we were 12 or over. Can she do this?"

Annie (13)

Admission to films is at the cinema manger's discretion. If you don't have proof and he/she doesn't believe you are the age you say, they do not have to let you in (even if you are the relevant age).
When films go onto video, they are reclassified (though many remain the same certificate). The classification is then marked on the video box, and you will be restricted according to your age.

If you are caught taking out a video that has an 18 certificate underage, you won't be fined but the shop could be.

EXTREME SPORTS

Like all dangerous activities, for many extreme sports, like diving, skiing and snowboarding, you need parental approval before you can attempt them. However, in practice this can only be enforced if you're on a recognised course or at a centre where you are insured against being injured.

If you attempt these sports on your own somewhere else, you do so at your own risk.

DRIVING

While the laws about driving cars and motorbikes apply only to public areas, roads and land, you'd be wise not to drive on private land if you have no knowledge of driving.

- If you are under 16, you cannot drive any vehicle, motorbike or car. Not even with an experienced driver by your side.
- At 16 years old, you can drive a moped.
- At 17 you can apply for a provisional license and start learning to drive a car, or motorbike.

Cars

Provisional licences are licences for learners and do not allow you to drive on the road alone. They are to enable you to learn to drive and you need to pass a test in order to receive a full licence.

The person teaching you to drive must be 21 or over and have had a licence for at least three years.

Motorbikes

You have two years to take your motorbike test from when you start learning to drive. While you can drive on the road with a provisional licence, you cannot ride a bike with more than a 125 cc engine, and you cannot take passengers.

FOOTBALL MATCHES

Thanks to the recent violent clashes at football matches, there are now fairly strict regulations governing what you can and can't do at a football match, on the way to a football match and on the way home.

- For a start, you cannot go onto the pitch or throw anything on or towards the pitch.
- You cannot take fireworks into a football game.
- You cannot be drunk, or get drunk at a match.
- You cannot have any alcohol with you.
- You cannot have a bottle of any kind with you.

TRAVELLING AND PASSPORTS

From birth everyone must now have their own passport to travel abroad. When you apply for a passport under the age of 16, your parents will have to make the application for you and this passport will only last for five years. After this time (and if you are 16), you will have to apply for a new passport and this time you will be issued with a 10 year one.

Travelling alone on a plane while under 16 is at the discretion of the airlines, and often children below the age of 14 will travel with airline chaperones.

As for package holidays, the majority of tour operators will not take under 16s without an adult present.

GAMBLING

Over 50% of teenagers gamble to some degree. This includes arcade games, electronic games, computer games and the horses and/or dogs. 3% of these people end up as serious gamblers which is why there are very strict rules and regulations about what you can and can't do on the gambling front.

The Lottery

• Under 16s are not allowed to play the lottery. If you do buy a ticket and win, you will not be allowed to collect any money.

Making bets and placing bets

• For starters under 18s cannot go into a betting shop, not even to place a bet for a parent.
• You cannot place a bet for yourself.
• You cannot collect a parent's/friend's/relative's winnings. It is an offence for an adult to wager a bet with you and/or get you to place a bet for them.

Bingo Halls

- You can go to a Bingo hall with an adult but you cannot play if you are under 18.

Arcades

- There are no specific rules governing arcades, however, due to public criticism, the majority now restrict under 16s from playing the slot machines.

Questions and answers

I bought a pair of shoes from this shop and after two weeks the heel broke. When I took them back they said I could have another pair or a credit note. My mum said they should give me my money back, but they said that wasn't their policy. Is this right?

Helen (14)

The law is very clear about consumer rights. It states that goods must be of satisfactory quality and fit for the purpose for which they are bought. If the heel of your shoe broke after two weeks and you'd been using them normally, they were not of satisfactory quality and therefore, your statutory (legal) rights say you are entitled to a refund. Shop policies cannot interfere with these rights and a shop cannot make you take a credit note or a new pair of shoes. Most shoe shops are covered by the Footwear Code of Practice, so if there is a discrepancy over whether the shoe was faulty, you can ask for the shoes to be sent to the Footwear Testing Centre for an independent opinion.

I want to go parachuting but my dad says no way. My friend knows of a place where they'll let anyone or any age do it. Does this mean I can go without his permission?

Lee (14)

No reputable, i.e. safe, qualified and experienced, parachuting instructor would allow an under 16 to parachute without parental consent. Apart from the fact that your parents have the right to know you are doing something potentially dangerous, there is also the insurance risk. This means it's unlikely an instructor would be insured to allow you to parachute. Therefore, if you did an illegal jump that caused you injury, you would probably not get compensation money.

INFORMATION AND ADVICE

Consumers Association
0645 123580

Small Claims Procedure
Lord Chancellor's Department
Civil Operations
Southside
105 Victoria Street
London SW1E 6QT
Tel: 0171 210 1689

Office of Fair Trading Consumer Information Line
0345 224499

For a series of free leaflets write to:
Office of Fair Trading
PO Box 2
Central Way
Feltham
Middlesex TW14 OTG
Tel: 0181 398 3405

Hairdressing Advisory Service
0891 517317

CHAPTER EIGHT

How Old?

We all know that age and maturity don't necessarily go hand in hand, which is why the law is flexible in certain areas. However, there are many areas where the law is not flexible, so it pays to know how old you need to be in order to do certain activities.

From age 5

Your parents have to make sure you are in full time education. You can be given alcohol in your home.

12

You can see a 12 certificate film. You can buy a pet.

13

You can get a part time job (subject to restrictions, see chapter 3).

14

You can work abroad as an actress/model (subject to restrictions, see chapter 3).
You can go to a bar (but not drink alcohol).

16

You can buy liqueur chocolates.
If you are a girl you can legally have sex (there is no age of consent for boys).
You can leave school and work full time.
You can get contraception without having to prove you're 'mature' enough to have sex.
You can probably leave home, with your parent's consent.
You can get married with your parent's consent.
You can say yes or no to medical treatment.
You can join a Youth Training Scheme.

You can legally buy cigarettes.
You can ask for an abortion without needing parental consent.
You can drink beer or cider in a restaurant.
You can apply for your own passport.

17

You can apply for a provisional licence to drive a car or motorbike.
You can take your driving test.
You can be interviewed by the police without your parents being there.

18

You can vote.
You can get married without parental consent.
A man can consent to homosexual sex with another man.
You can leave home.
You can join the army.
You can be sue and sued.
You can apply for a loan.
You can apply for a credit card.
You can make a will.
You can place a bet.
You can legally buy alcohol.
You can drink in a bar.
You can donate blood.
You can get a body piercing and tattoo without parental consent.

If you are adopted, you can apply for your adopted records.
You can buy fireworks.
You can change your name by deed poll.

21

You can teach someone to drive, as long as you have been driving for three years.
You can become an MP.
You can adopt a child.

AT ANY AGE

A savings account can be opened in your name.
You can make a complaint against a teacher/the police/any person in authority.
You can seek compensation.
You can take a faulty product back to a shop and demand a refund.

The Children's Legal Centre publish a full guide to your rights at different ages, called What Age Can I, *which is available from them.*

Where to go for help

If you need information or advice about any aspect of the law, contact one of the addresses below. Useful addresses are also listed at the end of each chapter.

England and Wales
The Children's Legal Centre
University of Essex
Wivenhoe Park
Colchester
Essex CO4 3SQ
Tel: 01206 873820

Scotland
Scottish Children's Law Centre
Cranston House
108 Argyle Street
Glasgow
Tel: 0800 317 500

Northern Ireland
Children's Law Centre, Northern Ireland
101 University Street
Belfast BT7 1HB
Tel: 01232 245704

Republic of Ireland
Children's Rights Alliance
4 Christchurch Square
Dublin 8
Tel: (01) 453 0355

* * *

Law Society (for a list of solicitors and their specialities)
113 Chancery Lane
London WC2A 1PL
Tel: 0171 242 1222

Law Centres Federation
Duchess House
18–19 Warren Street,
London W1P 5DB
Tel: 0171 387 8570

European Commission of Human Rights
Council of Europe
F-67075
Strabourg
Cedex
France

National Youth Agency
17–23 Albion Street
Leicester LE1 6GD
Tel: 0116 285 6789

Youthaid
409 Brixton Road
London SW9 7DQ
Tel: 0171 737 8068

Glossary

ADOPTIVE PARENTS
Those who have been given legal responsibility over you in law.

AGE OF CONSENT
The age when it is legal for a girl to agree to have sex.

APPEAL
The process where you can have a decision reviewed by a higher court.

ARRESTED
This means the police have charged you with a criminal offence and you have to be kept in their custody until a court hearing has taken place.

BIRTH PARENTS
Your biological mother and father.

BY-LAWS
Regulations made by the local authority not the central government. They are local laws, particular to the area in which you live.

COMMON LAW
Law based on custom and previous cases.

COMPETENT
Able to understand what is going on.

CONSUMER
The person who uses an article produced.

DIVORCE
The legal end of a marriage.

EXCLUDED
Not allowed at school for a certain period of time.

EXPELLED
Thrown out of a school and not allowed to return.

HALF BROTHER AND HALF SISTER
The children one of your parents has with another person. You are related to them by law and by blood.

GROSS INDECENCY
This is where a person tries to get an under 16 to touch them indecently i.e. genital touching.

HARASS
To worry and annoy repeatedly.

INDECENT ASSAULT
This is everything that stops short of penetrative sex e.g. touching the genital area and breasts, rubbing up to a person, forced oral sex. It can be committed by a man or a woman. Often women who have sex with boys under 16 are charged with this.

INCEST
This occurs when members of the same close family have a sexual relationship.

INDECENT EXPOSURE
This occurs when a man exposes his penis to a woman.

INDUSTRIAL TRIBUNAL
An independent board not linked to the courts which makes judgements in disputes between employers and employees (e.g. sexual harassment, unfair dismissal).

INTIMIDATION
The use of violence or threats to make someone do something.

INTOXICATION
Being drunk and out of control.

LOITERING
Hanging about in a particular place for no apparent reason.

PETITION
An application form asking for a divorce to be granted.

PROSECUTED
Taken to court for breaking the law.

RAPE
Sexual intercourse without consent.

SEPARATE
No longer live together as husband and wife.

SEXUAL ABUSE
Sexual attention without consent, e.g. being touched sexually, being asked to touch someone, being forced to look at indecent material, pose for indecent material, being forced to have vaginal or anal intercourse.

SOCIAL SERVICES
The public bodies responsible for carrying out welfare work.

STEP PARENT
If either of your parents chooses to marry again, step parent is another name for their new wife/husband in relation to you.

STEPBROTHERS AND STEPSISTERS
The children from your step parent's first marriage/relationship.

STATUTORY RIGHTS
Legal rights.

SUMMONS
An official letter that tells you you must attend a court on a particular date and at a particular time.

UNDERAGE SEX
Sex before you reach the age of consent.

Index

ORDER FORM
Wise Guides

0 340 75297 1	DIVORCE & SEPARATION	£3.99
0 340 75299 8	SELF-ESTEEM	£3.99
0 340 63604 1	PERIODS	£3.99
0 340 69973 6	DRUGS	£3.99
0 340 71483 2	BULLYING	£3.99
0 340 71042 X	SEX	£3.99

All Hodder Children's books are available at your local bookshop or newsagent, or can be ordered direct from the publisher. Just tick the titles you want and fill in the form below. Prices and availability subject to change without notice.

Hodder Children's Books, Cash Sales Department, Bookpoint, 39 Milton Park, Abingdon, Oxon, OX14 4TD, UK. If you have a credit card you may order by telephone – (01235) 400414.

Please enclose a cheque or postal order made payable to Bookpoint Ltd to the value of the cover price and allow the following for postage and packing:

UK & BFPO – £1.00 for the first book, 50p for the second book, and 30p for each additional book ordered, up to a maximum charge of £3.00.

OVERSEAS & EIRE – £2.00 for the first book, £1.00 for the second book, and 50p for each additional book.

Name ....

Address ....

....

....

If you would prefer to pay by credit card, please complete the following:

Please debit my Visa/Access/Diner's Card/American Express (delete as applicable) card no:

----- ----- ----- ----- ----- ----- ----- ----- ----- ----- ----- ----- ----- ----- ----- -----

Signature ....

Expiry Date ....